50

John +
110 The
Whe

C000016271

DN2 5SN

Branch Lines of
Somerset

Branch Lines of Somerset

COLIN G. MAGGS

ALAN SUTTON

First published in the United Kingdom in 1993 by
Alan Sutton Publishing Ltd · Phoenix Mill · Stroud · Gloucestershire

First published in the United States of America in 1993 by
Alan Sutton Publishing Inc. · 83 Washington Street · Dover NH 03820

British Library Cataloguing in Publication Data

Maggs, Colin G.
Branch Lines of Somerset
I. Title
385.09423

ISBN 0–7509–0226–4

Library of Congress Cataloging in Publication data applied for

Jacket photographs. Front: Ivatt class 2MT 2–6–2T no. 41216 at Highbridge, having arrived
with a train from Evercreech Junction. To the left a train is ready to return to Evercreech
Junction, while on the right is the locomotive shed and the buildings of the former railway works. (*c.* 1961 M.E.J. Deane.) *Back:* 55XX class 2–6–2 No. 5571 leaves Crowcombe
for Minehead. (*c.* 1960 M.E.J. Deane.)

Endpapers. Front: 64XX class 0–6–0PT No.6412 reaches the head of the 1 in 91 gradient up
to Blue Anchor, hauling the 10.35 a.m. from Minehead. *Back:* 43XX class 2–6–0 No. 6398
leaves Blue Anchor with a Taunton to Minehead train.

Typeset in 9/10 Palatino.
Typesetting and origination by
Alan Sutton Publishing Limited.
Printed and bound in Great Britain by
WBC, Bridgend, Mid Glam.

Contents

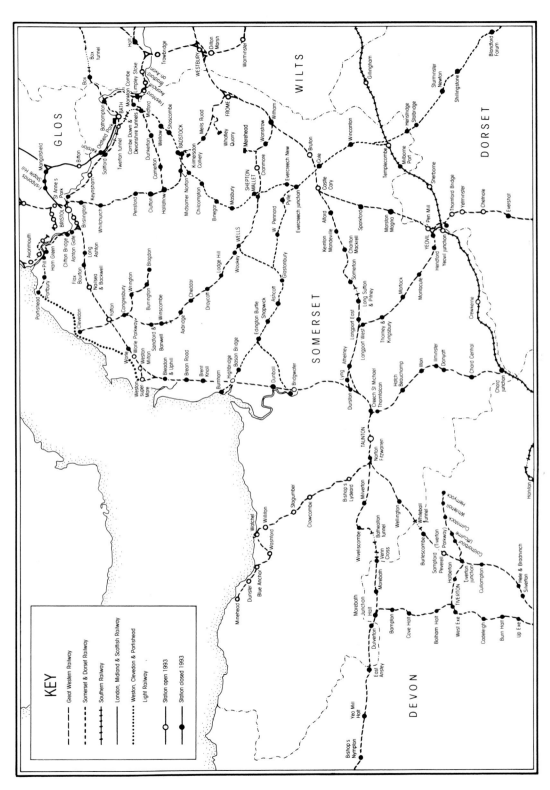

BRANCH LINES OF SOMERSET

Introduction

The railway map of Somerset shows the two Great Western Railway main lines to Taunton: the original route via Bristol and the direct route to the West via Castle Cary. Linking the two was the Wilts, Somerset and Weymouth Railway which left the London to Bristol line at Bathampton, just east of Bath, and proceeded to Westbury, where one line ran to Salisbury and the other to Weymouth.

The other two main lines through the county were the Somerset and Dorset Railway on its way from Bath to Bournemouth, and the London and South Western Railway's Salisbury to Exeter line, which followed the county's southern boundary.

The first Somerset section of the GWR to be opened was between Bristol and Bath in 1840; the final length of the line, that through Box Tunnel between Bath and Chippenham, being opened the following year. 1841 also saw the westwards extension of the GWR, known as the Bristol and Exeter Railway. Although an independent company, it was closely associated with the GWR, sharing the same engineer, I.K. Brunel. Bridgwater was reached in 1841, Taunton in 1842, Beambridge (eight and a half miles west of the county town) in 1843, and Exeter in 1844. The B&ER was absorbed by the GWR from 1 January 1876.

Both the GWR and the B&ER were built to the broad gauge of 7 ft $0^{1}/_{4}$ in, but as Britain's railway system developed and through running was necessary, the broad gauge lines were gradually converted to mixed gauge to avoid the trouble and expense of transferring passengers and goods at a break of gauge. This came into use between Bath and Bristol in 1874, to Taunton the following year and onwards to Exeter in 1876. The broad gauge was withdrawn completely on 20 May 1892.

The Wilts, Somerset and Weymouth Railway opened in piecemeal fashion. Thingley Junction, just west of Chippenham, to Westbury opened in 1848, Frome was reached in 1850, Yeovil in 1856 and Weymouth in 1857, the line from Bathampton to Bradford-on-Avon being opened the same year. The WSWR had been transferred to the GWR in 1851, and was converted to standard gauge in 1874.

Around the turn of the century, the Westbury to Castle Cary section of the former WSWR became part of the GWR's new route to the west. A new line was built between Patney, Chirton and Westbury to avoid the detour via Devizes; and another new line constructed in order to link Castle Cary with Langport. The new line opened to through trains in 1906, and was further improved by the opening of the Westbury and Frome avoiding lines in 1933, enabling each through express to save about three minutes.

The Somerset and Dorset Railway also had a complicated history. It was an amalgam of two companies: the broad gauge Somerset Central Railway, and the standard gauge Dorset Central Railway, which by 1863 ran between Burnham-on-Sea and Poole. Although an admirable achievement, there were not large numbers of passengers wishing to travel between these two stations, and its only hope of prosperity was seen to be in the building of an extension over the Mendips, from Evercreech Junction to Bath, there linking with the Midland Railway's branch from Mangotsfield which had opened in 1869. This S&DR extension opened in 1874, and from this date the Bath to Bournemouth section became the main line, the Burnham to Evercreech Junction section being relegated to secondary status.

In 1859 the London and South Western Railway extended its line from Salisbury as far as Gillingham, and onwards to Exeter the following year.

The branches are described in the same order as the main lines which serve them.

Grateful thanks are due to E.J.M. Hayward for checking and improving the text and captions.

Key to Maps

———	GREAT WESTERN RAILWAY
⊥⊥⊥⊥	WESTON, CLEVEDON AND PORTISHEAD LIGHT RAILWAY
△△△	MIDLAND RAILWAY/LONDON MIDLAND AND SCOTTISH RAILWAY
✗✗✗	SOMERSET AND DORSET JOINT RAILWAY
┼┼┼┼┼	LONDON AND SOUTH WESTERN RAILWAY/SOUTHERN RAILWAY
....	INDUSTRIAL RAILWAY

Bristol to Frome

Although in more recent times the branch was operated as an entity, it originally consisted of two distinct sections.

The first railway to reach Radstock was the Wilts, Somerset and Weymouth Railway's branch from Frome. This enabled the company to tap lucrative coal traffic, which hitherto had been served by the rather inadequate Somerset Coal Canal tramway. Because of difficulties experienced in obtaining land, the line was not opened until 14 November 1854, although planned in 1844, by which time the GWR had taken over the WSWR. Constructed to the broad gauge, initially only coal traffic was carried.

Having thus projected a railway into the coalfield, it was thought profitable to continue the line northwards to link with the GWR's main line at Keynsham or Bristol, tapping further collieries en route.

The first turf of the Bristol and North Somerset Railway, as this extension was called, was turned at Clutton on 7 October 1863. Following this auspicious occasion the company was beset with financial difficulties, and in 1870 its image was not helped when the company's secretary, J. Bingham, who had run up huge bills for legal and Parliamentary expenses, was sentenced to twelve months' imprisonment with hard labour for attempting to defraud W.M. Baillie, a Bristol banker.

The financial difficulties caused no less than six contractors to be employed over the ten years it took to complete the line. Its most impressive and expensive engineering feature was Pensford Viaduct constructed of stone and with a length of 995 ft. The railway was carried on sixteen arches of 50 ft span and 95 ft in height. At the time of writing, the BR Property Board is offering this Grade II structure for sale at £1.

The standard gauge BNSR was opened on 3 September 1873, creating a break of gauge at Radstock. As this was obviously inconvenient, the broad gauge Radstock to Frome line was narrowed on 18 June 1874, but not adapted for passenger traffic until 5 July 1875. Latterly, the principal passenger train over the branch was the 5.55 p.m. from Frome. Consisting of two coaches, its tank engine carried express headlights. It provided a connection between the Frome stop of the 'Up' Channel Islands boat train and Bristol, and only called at Radstock and Pensford. The route was also used on summer Saturdays by through expresses carrying holiday-makers from Birmingham to Weymouth. Competition from road transport led to the line being closed to passengers from 2 November 1959, but the profitable goods and mineral traffic continued. Coal was taken from Radstock to Portishead Power Station and Imperial Smelting Processes Limited at Avonmouth, and traffic also ran to and from Marcroft's wagon works, Radstock. At Mells Road was a bitumen terminal, and, two miles short of Frome, a private line served Whatley Quarry.

In order to effect maintenance economies, it was decided to split the branch into two sections, and on 25 April 1966 the two and a half mile length from Kilmersdon Sidings, east of Radstock, to Mells Road was closed. Fortunately the track was not lifted, and when a flood washed away part of the Bristol to Radstock line on 10 July 1968, that section was closed permanently, while that from Radstock to Mells Road was reopened, causing coal to take a very roundabout route to Portishead and Avonmouth.

The last load of coal brought to the surface at Writhlington on 28 September 1973 marked the end of Radstock coalfield. Marcroft's wagon works still operated, and continued to function until 29 June 1988 when the branch was cut back to Hapsford Loop, though this section of line has now been reopened as a preserved line by the Somerset and Avon Railway Association.

The Bristol to Frome branch was notable for the number of industrial lines feeding it. Pensford Colliery, three-quarters of a mile south of Pensford station, was sited about 100 ft above the level of the GWR. An agreement was signed on 9 September 1910 for a self-acting incline, terminating at the pithead. As this layout would have made working difficult, plans were amended on 15 March 1911 to make the incline longer and less steep, with the method of working changed from self-acting to haulage engine. The 400-yd incline was constructed and open by 1912, but until 1917 when the colliery came into full use, it is likely that a greater tonnage was hauled up the incline than lowered down it.

On the west side of the BNSR was a loop, from which two sidings ran uphill to the south for holding empty wagons; another two sidings running downhill to the north for loaded wagons. Both pairs of sidings had a capacity of about forty-three wagons each. A spur was provided for each pair so that shunting operations could take place independent from working over the main line.

A short rake of empty trucks was allowed to run by gravity across a diamond crossing at the foot of the incline, momentum causing them to run up into another siding. From there, the wagons were run singly to the foot of the incline. Here a wagon's coupling chain was hooked to the steel cable taken from a wagon just descended, a hawser being looped round the leading axle and also hooked to the cable as a safety precaution in the event of the coupling chain breaking. When all was ready, the shunter at the foot of the incline gave a ring on the bell signal from his hut to the incline winding house at the summit. On arrival at the head of the incline, empty wagons were run back by gravity into the pithead sidings while still attached to the cable.

A loaded wagon was hauled from the pithead sidings to the head of the incline and lowered to its foot, where it was unhooked and allowed to gravitate to the lower sidings. It is believed that there was only one accident on the incline, this occurring about 1917 when a wagon became detached from the cable, was derailed on the diamond crossing and rolled over three times. This incline was capable of dispatching up to eight loaded wagons an hour, though the normal daily traffic was about thirty 10-ton wagons. Another incident, though not affecting the incline, was in December 1946 when the dirt batch slipped and buried the GWR branch, which could not be reopened until March 1947.

To ensure the safe working of the incline, the National Coal Board issued instructions to its staff:

1. On no account must wagons be sent down the Incline unless the signal at the top is set at 'clear'.
2. Not more than one loaded wagon or one empty wagon may be allowed to travel upon the Incline at any single journey, either up or down, and every wagon, loaded or empty, must have the safety rope attached to the axle of the wagon in addition to the ordinary coupling attached to the rope.

3. The Engineman shall not start the upward journey until he has received the proper Signal from the Shunter in charge at the bottom.

4. The Engineman shall not lower a journey until he has received the proper Signal from the Shunter at the bottom that he is in charge of the Catch Points.

5. The Shunter at the top shall signal to the Shunter at the bottom when the journey is ready to be sent down the Incline.

Although Pensford was the second largest pit in Somerset, an above average number of stationary haulage engines was required underground owing to the rise and fall of the seams due to faulting, making the pit expensive to work. Because it was uneconomic to modernize, the pit was closed, the last coal being raised on 13 December 1958.

Two mineral branches diverged at Clutton: one ran parallel with the main line for half a mile before branching off to Fry's Bottom Colliery. This line opened in 1876 and closed 31 July 1895. The other, about three-quarters of a mile in length, curved eastwards up to Greyfield Colliery, not far from the present A39 road. This siding, opened in 1876 and closed in 1911, was worked by an 0–4–0ST, though initially gravity was employed, horses drawing the empty wagons up to the colliery. The GWR was responsible for the maintenance of both these colliery branches.

North of Farrington Gurney halt was another mining complex: Farrington Colliery to the west and Springfield Colliery to the east, both served by standard gauge lines; a narrow gauge tramway from Old Mills Colliery carrying coal to Springfield Colliery. The Farrington branch opened in 1882 with horse traction, but was later worked by various 0–4–0STs until closure in October 1921. The Springfield line was worked with horses until October 1940, when a Ruston & Hornsby four-wheel diesel-mechanical shunter was brought into use. It, with a similar successor, ran until the colliery's closure on 1 April 1966.

When the S&DJR closed on 6 March 1966 a cord line was built, linking it at Radstock to the former BNSR so that coal could still be removed from Writhlington Colliery, this pit remaining open until 19 November 1973.

East of Radstock station was Ludlow's Colliery, served by a broad gauge branch from 1854. For ninety-nine years the yard was shunted by horses, then, early in 1953, the surface was adapted to permit shunting by road tractor equipped with buffer beam and wagon couplings. On 19 March the colliery closed!

Kilmersdon Colliery, to the south and above the main line, was connected to it from 1878 by a standard gauge line. Its length totalling half a mile, the line was approximately flat from the pit, crossed the Radstock to Kilmersdon road on the level and ended in an inclined plane some 500 ft in length on a gradient of 1 in 8, taking it down to the valley and the GWR. Until 1896 the length of track at the top of the incline was worked by horses, but that year locomotive operation began, and from 10 September 1929 until closure in 1973, Peckett 0–4–0ST Works No. 1788 was usually in charge of operations.

The method of working was to push five or six wagons over the weighbridge in order that a bill of lading could be written, an orange light indicating when the next wagon was required to be moved on to the weighbridge. This task completed, No. 1788 pushed the wagons over an ungated level crossing, through a shallow cutting and on to an embankment with fields on either side. To prevent wagons and the locomotive accidentally plunging down the incline, a metal stop block was placed across the rails.

The first wagon was uncoupled and hooked to a wire cable, which passed round a horizontal winding drum and led down to the bottom of the incline where it was fastened to an empty wagon. Everything ready, the warning bell was rung, the stop block moved aside and the loaded wagon descended, dragging up the empty, the two passing mid-way.

Between the tracks at the head of the incline, two levers controlled the band brakes on the drum in the winding house. Immediately the empty wagon reached the head of the incline, a lever was pulled to place a stop block across the rails, and No. 1788 shunted the wagon to a siding, pushing another loaded wagon to the head of the incline.

Meanwhile, the first loaded wagon, at the foot of the incline, had its brake applied just before the rope stopped so that it was slack and could be uncoupled. The wagon then rolled by gravity round a sharp curve to a siding parallel with, but at a lower level than, the Frome branch, from where it was taken by a main-line locomotive. In the 1960s about fifty wagons were removed daily.

On the arrival of a train of empty wagons, the shunter at the foot of the incline went along the train uncoupling the wagons and recoupling with a 'D' link, adjoining the middle link of each three-link wagon coupling. This gave sufficient play to avoid buffer locking on the sharp curve at the foot of the incline.

The 'D' link was composed of a letter C-shaped bar and a movable shank. As each 'D' link came between the first and second truck, a cord was attached by the shunter to the shank and, as the first truck went up the incline, the trucks behind it were drawn forward. When they had moved far enough the cord was pulled, resulting in the 'D' link and its pin falling to the ground.

From Mells Road station the two mile long Newbury Railway branched off to Mells Colliery, Vobster Quarry and Newbury Colliery. Originally constructed to the broad gauge, it was converted in 1874. The line was horse-worked from its opening in 1857 until the introduction of locomotives around the turn of the century. The three users formed a committee and normally each undertaking used its own locomotive. If, however, one of the engines failed, the committee's traffic manager pooled the remaining locomotives to cover the gap.

Newbury Colliery closed in 1927, Mells in 1943, while stone ceased to be moved from Vobster Quarry about 1965–6. The line continued to be used at its Mells Road end to give access to a bitumen terminal, this traffic ceasing by 1978. A short distance to the east of the Newbury Railway, between 1925 and 1933 it was paralleled by a branch from the GWR to Bilboa Quarry, but in about 1934 a connection was made from the quarry to the Newbury Railway.

In 1893 Somerset Stone Quarries, two miles west of Frome, made an agreement with the GWR to be served by a siding. This, in turn, was served by a 2 ft 3 in gauge tramway, worked by horses initially, but from 1907 onwards by two Kerr, Stuart and Co. Ltd 0–4–0STs. In the early 1930s, the system was incorporated with the New Frome Quarry's 2 ft gauge system. In 1943 this was superseded by a 2 mile long standard gauge line through the highly picturesque Vallis Vale to Whatley Quarry. At first worked by conventional industrial locomotives, from 1947 onwards trains were hauled by four-wheel geared Sentinels with a vertical boiler sited in the cab. From 1963 four-wheel diesel-hydraulics built by Thomas Hill were introduced, and for the trip to Whatley a pair were run back-to-back.

In the early 1960s, the line was modified to allow BR wagons to work through to Whatley, instead of the stone having to be transhipped from internal use wagons. At the same time a nine track marshalling yard was brought into use. In 1973 a new one and a half mile long deviation line with three new tunnels totalling 649 yds, was built to enable BR locomotives to run to Whatley, and it was opened on 9 September 1974. In 1990 ARC, owners of the quarry, bought four Class 59/1, General Motors diesels named after local villages. They were crewed by BR for running over Nationalized lines. ARC has its own shunter *Pride of Whatley*, and in 1992 while it was out of service, the Swindon and Cricklade Railway loaned its ex-BR Class 25 D5222.

An interesting feature of the Radstock branch was that passengers boarding at Farrington Gurney halt had to buy their tickets at the Miners' Arms public house. One mother getting on at the halt in the dark and burdened with pram and child, was assisted into the van by a kindly guard. While carrying out his good deed, he accidentally turned his handlamp to green. The train left for Midsomer Norton with the guard still on the platform. He went to the Miners' Arms and phoned Midsomer Norton station, requesting a taxi.

Tonnage of Coal Dispatched

Station	1903	1913	1933
Pensford	2,553	26,656	31,061
Clutton	98,092	51,090	-
Farrington	111,474	81,753	40,878
Radstock	129,125	146,079	64,036
Mells Road	33,494	60,187	32,204

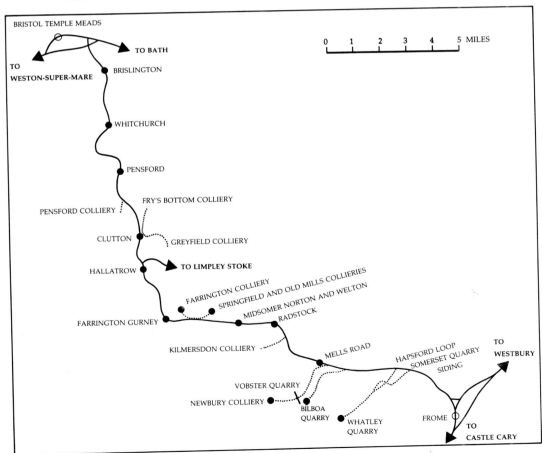

The ceremony of cutting the first sod of the Bristol and North Somerset Railway on 7 October 1863. This was performed by Mrs Milward, wife of Prebendary Milward, the latter an active promoter of the undertaking.

Illustrated London News

55XX class 2–6–2T No. 5536 at Brislington with a Bristol (Temple Meads) to Frome train. Coal wagons stand in the loop siding, left. At the rear of the train the line descends towards North Somerset Junction, where the London main line via Bath is joined.

22.5.59 R.J. Sellick

Many country stations had attractive gardens, and sometimes their names were picked out in topiary or whitened stones. Here is an example of the latter at Brislington.

c. 1910 M.J. Tozer Collection

An empty wagon starting its ascent to Pensford Colliery. Loaded wagons were run into the sidings on the right.

8.9.53 Author

Permanent way men have left their motor trolley on this special spur at Chelwood Bridge, while carrying out maintenance nearby.

21.2.50 Author

Ex-ROD class 2–8–0 No. 3011 at Fry's Bottom, Clutton, with 'Up' empties. It has stopped at the board so that the wagon brakes can be pinned down before descending the incline.

17.9.53 Author

57XX class 0–6–0PT No. 8744 enters Hallatrow with the 2.53 p.m. Saturdays-only Bristol (Temple Meads) to Frome. The BNSR station building is similar to that at Brislington.

23.5.59 Hugh Ballantyne

Passengers at Farrington Gurney Halt bought their tickets beneath the water tank at the Miners' Arms.

D.E. Mullins

A friendly porter gives schoolchildren a ride on the platform barrow, Midsomer Norton and Welton station.

1933 Author

Wagon near the top of the inclined plane on the Kilmersdon Colliery branch, Radstock. A loaded wagon descending on the line nearest the camera drew this one up empty.

W.H. Harbor / Author's Collection

8750 class 0–6–0PT No. 3735 between Midsomer Norton and Radstock with the 10.17 a.m. Bristol (Temple Meads) to Frome. It is about to pass under the S&DR's Bath to Bournemouth line. Notice the fixed distant signal.

10.10.59 Hugh Ballantyne

55XX class 2–6–2T No. 5446 with a Bristol (Temple Meads) to Frome train passing over one of the notorious level crossings at Radstock which held up traffic. A few yards to the right was the S & DR level crossing. The signalman just visible on the right waits to collect the tablet.

M.E.J. Deane

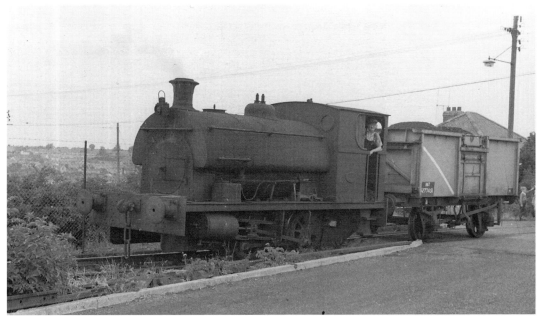

Peckett 0–4–0ST Works No. 1788, at Kilmersdon Colliery. This engine is now preserved by the Somerset and Dorset Trust at Washford on the West Somerset Railway.

24.7.62 Rev. Alan Newman

Four-wheeled Sentinel Works No. 9398 of 1950, belonging to Vobster Quarry, at the Roads Reconstruction tar works near Mells Road. This geared locomotive had the general appearance of a diesel engine, and with its fast-revving engine, also had its sound. The vertical boiler was concealed in the cab, while under the bonnet were cylinders and gearing.

20.7.54 Rev. Alan Newman

Roads Reconstruction No. 3, another vertical-boilered Sentinel, arrives at Hapsford from Whatley Quarry with loaded side-tipping wagons. The late Ivo Peters, noted railway photographer, leans from the cab and other members of the Bath Railway Society are within. This locomotive is preserved at Welsh Mills Children's Adventure Playground, Frome.

9.5.59 Rev. Alan Newman

An older vertical-boilered Sentinel is Works No. 6090 of 1925, notable for being shown at the Wembley Exhibition of that year.

27.6.63 Rev. Alan Newman

Hallatrow to Limpley Stoke

Although the Somerset Coal Canal ran along the Cam Valley from Paulton Basin to a junction with the Kennet and Avon Canal at Dundas Aqueduct near Limpley Stoke, this waterway was far from ideal for transporting coal. Apart from the usual problems of water shortage in summer, and the canal freezing in winter, a staircase of twenty-two locks near Combe Hay added to the expense of working. Following the completion of the Bristol and North Somerset Railway to Radstock, that company built a branch from Hallatrow to Camerton to tap this coal traffic. The station at Hallatrow needed considerable improvements to raise it to junction status. The single platform was insufficient and another through platform and a terminal bay platform were added, while a new signal box controlled the more complex layout.

Although the Board of Trade Inspector passed the line on 31 May 1881, in practice there was little point in taking this step because no colliery company had applied for rail access, and the anticipated low volume of general goods and passenger traffic would not have covered expenses.

The line, worked by the GWR, opened to goods and passenger traffic on 1 March 1882, the GWR absorbing the BNSR just over two years later on 1 July 1884.

A great disadvantage was that the branch fell on a gradient of 1 in 47 from Hallatrow to Camerton. This meant that the grade was against the load, limiting coal trains to fifteen wagons. Because 'Down' goods trains could be longer than those in the 'Up' direction, the timetable offered five passenger, one mixed and one goods in the 'Down' direction, and three passenger, one mixed and three goods the opposite way. As the passenger service was unbalanced, when the four wheel coach needed to be returned to Hallatrow, it was sent back empty at the rear of a goods train.

The opening of the branch caused such a serious decline in the tonnage conveyed by the Somerset Coal Canal that its income was insufficient to meet expenses, and the undertaking closed in 1898. Five years later it was sold to the GWR for £2,000, a substantial part of the Limpley Stoke and Camerton Railway being built on its course. A new line was necessary because a colliery, the largest in the county, was being opened at Dunkerton, and the existing line with its limit of fifteen wagons was thought to be totally inadequate. The new line had a gradient of 1 in 100 in favour of loaded trains, which could consist of up to fifty trucks, though it is believed that in the event no train of this length was ever run.

Messrs Pauling and Company, Westminster, won the contract and opened the section from Camerton to Dunkerton Colliery in 1907. A steam navvy was employed filling wagons with slag at Camerton Colliery to provide material for the construction of an embankment. The seven mile long section from Dunkerton to Limpley Stoke included several interesting engineering features. The first was the impressive 78 yd long Dunkerton viaduct, while three shorter ones at Midford totalled 153 yds. The 66 yd long canal tunnel at Combe Hay was underpinned on its south side, the masonry refaced and made fit for trains. A canal footbridge at Monkton Combe, which had been cast at Paulton in 1811, was raised and adapted to span the railway.

The line opened on 9 May 1910, the five passenger trains each way taking a minimum of 32 minutes to cover the $11^1/_2$ miles between Hallatrow and Limpley Stoke. The train was usually a third class only railmotor car which was stabled overnight at Radstock and worked a shuttle service, two trains continuing to Trowbridge. The passenger service was withdrawn on 22 March 1915 as a wartime economy measure. Some found the bus service inconvenient and an experimental service, excluding Midford Halt, was re-instated on 9 July 1923, only to be withdrawn finally on 21 September 1925. This was not quite the final passenger train, as in the summer of 1926 or 1927, Monkton Combe School chartered a railmotor for an excursion to Saltford Regatta. As the section of line from Camerton to Hallatrow was not really needed after closure to passenger services, in order to economize, freight services were withdrawn from this section on 8 February 1932 and the rails lifted.

Three or four coal trains and a goods train ran daily until Dunkerton and Priston collieries closed, then one train daily sufficed as Camerton was the only pit remaining open. This colliery closed in 1950 and after that date trains averaged less than one a month. The last goods ran on 14 February 1951.

The wooden permanent way huts set beside the line every one and a half miles were left unlocked by gangers. Colliers gathered inside at weekends, and if the huts were locked they broke the doors open. Inside they inverted a bucket, threw a newspaper over it to make a cloth and played cards. Each Monday morning, the ganger always made sure he had a sackful of wooden keys which wedged the running rails in the chairs, because the miners kicked them out to burn on their fire in the permanent way huts. The permanent way men got their own back by emptying the snares that the colliers set for rabbits before they could reach them, the permanent way men taking turns to have a rabbit. Between Midford and Combe Hay big filberts grew beside the line and the men often picked a hatful. In season blackberries or mushrooms could be gathered so the men frequently had something to take home.

One summer's day, as a permanent way trolley approached Combe Hay Tunnel, the men were astounded to see that there were no rails in it. A closer look revealed that there were, but they were covered with sheep, which had squeezed through the fence and found it a cool place to rest.

At one time a porter at Camerton was keen on going to dances at Combe Hay. Believing it better to travel in style, and knowing where the key of the hand-propelled gangers' trolley was kept, he used the trolley to travel to his evening's entertainment. He locked it to the rails while dancing and then returned home on it afterwards. A pump trolley was used unofficially for giving children lifts home from Monkton Combe village school to outlying houses. One girl who lived at the Viaduct Hotel, between Monkton Combe and Limpley Stoke, was given a regular ride.

About six Red Cross coaches stood at Dunkerton Sidings for three to four months before the invasion of Normandy in 1944. Periodically they were run up and down to prevent the bearings seizing. During the Second World War an LMS 0–6–0 sometimes worked branch trains.

The line was popular with film producers. In 1931 *The Ghost Train* was shot at Camerton, and this led to publicity folders being distributed to cinema audiences: 'See the Ghost Train Country'. In 1937 some of the night scenes for the Edgar Wallace thriller *Kate Plus Ten* were shot on the tracks of the disused colliery at Dunkerton, while in 1952 the branch formed the setting for *The Titfield Thunderbolt*.

Tonnage of coal sent from Camerton:	1903	87,315
	1913	57,790
	1933	27,676

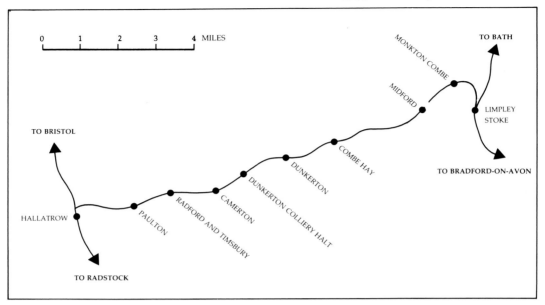

Notice of closing of Dunkerton station as a wartime economy measure.

Constructing the Camerton to Limpley Stoke line west of Midford viaduct. Notice the steam excavator, left, at the end of the cutting. Spoil from this cutting will be used to make the embankment beyond. The track is contractor's, rather than permanent way. The viaduct in the background carries the Somerset and Dorset Joint Railway's Bath to Radstock line.

c. 1909 Author's Collection

The closed Camerton and Limpley Stoke line passes along the Cam Valley: the track was to remain another three years before being lifted. On the hillside beyond, the 'Up' 'Pines Express', hauled by a Class 2P 4–4–0 and a BR Standard Class 5, passes Midford station.

10.3.55 Hugh Ballantyne

The Camerton to Limpley Stoke line was partly built on the defunct Somerset Coal Canal. The ironwork of this footbridge at Monkton Combe was cast at Paulton in 1811 and is seen here spanning the derelict canal. It was recycled and used for bridging the railway at the same spot.

c. 1907 Author's Collection

The Monkton Combe footbridge in railway use, supported on engineer's blue bricks instead of stone. Notice Limpley Stoke fixed distant signal.

1952 T.J. Saunders

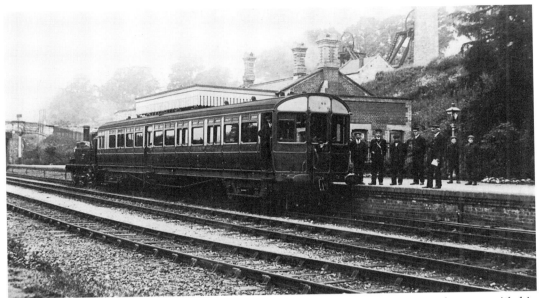

An 0–4–2T and auto trailer No. 54 at Camerton. The railmotor conductor can be seen with his money bag and ticket pouch.

c. 1910 M.J. Tozer Collection

Arthur Gerrish on a 'dolly' at Monkton Combe West ground frame. Working the handles and pedals propelled it. Porter Bert Gane stands in the background.

1946 Author's Collection

Lion, alias *Thunderbolt* and Collett 0–4–2T No. 1401 in Monkton Combe yard, for the filming of *The Titfield Thunderbolt*.

June 1952 T.J. Saunders

Collett 0–4–2T No. 1401 with ex-Wisbech and Upwell Tramway coach No. 7, at Monkton Combe during filming of *The Titfield Thunderbolt*.

23.6.52 Author

View from the veranda of the rail lifting train brake van, being pushed between Midford and Combe Hay.

28.5.58 Author

Track lifting east of Combe Hay.

28.5.59 Author

Bristol Harbour Railway

The Bristol Harbour Railway, opened on 11 March 1872, was built jointly by the Bristol and Exeter Railway, the GWR and Bristol Corporation. Leaving the main Bristol to Bath line just east of Temple Meads, it was a highly expensive branch requiring the demolition of a vicarage and the cutting of a 292 yd long tunnel through a burial ground, involving the expense of exhumation and re-interment of bodies. The branch also required a long viaduct and three bridges. The most interesting of the latter was the opening bascule bridge over Bathurst Basin. Designed by Charles Richardson, pupil of I.K. Brunel and later to be appointed chief engineer of the Severn tunnel, he also invented the sprung handled cricket bat. Bathurst Bridge accommodated mixed gauge, and was powered by a horizontal steam engine built in the city by the Avonside Engine Company in 1872. It is now preserved in the Bristol Industrial Museum, not far from the bridge. A friction drive was provided to prevent the bridge from being overdriven. On 12 June 1876 the branch was extended half a mile to Wapping wharf, and on 4 October 1906 extended yet again to link with the Portishead branch at Ashton Junction.

Although normally a goods-only line, it was used on occasions as a diversion when the main line was blocked, as happened on Sundays 26 April and 15 November 1931, when two over-line bridges were demolished in order to quadruple the main line at Parson Street.

Following the rundown of the city docks, the line east of Wapping wharf closed on 6 January 1964, and in more recent years traffic has been withdrawn from the Ashton junction to Wapping wharf line.

The preserved Peckett 0–6–0ST *Henbury* beside the New Cut, drawing hopper wagons to Wapping Wharf while on hire to the Western Fuel Company.

16.10.81 Author's Collection

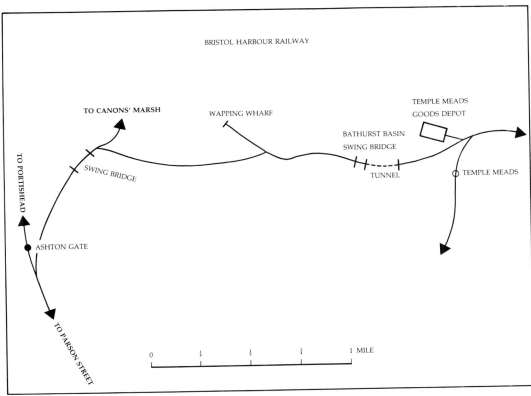

BRISTOL HARBOUR RAILWAY

TO CANONS' MARSH

WAPPING WHARF

TEMPLE MEADS
GOODS DEPOT

BATHURST BASIN
SWING BRIDGE

TO PORTISHEAD

SWING BRIDGE

TUNNEL

TEMPLE MEADS

ASHTON GATE

TO PARSON STREET

0   ¼   ½   ¾   1 MILE

8750 class 0–6–0PT No. 3650 (of 82B, St Philip's Marsh, Bristol shed and now preserved at Didcot Railway Centre), on Bathurst bascule bridge. The third rail bearer for the broad gauge is arrowed, left. Each time the bridge needed to be moved, the water pipe to Wapping Goods Yard had to be disconnected.

Port of Bristol Authority

Bristol to Portishead

The history of the Portishead branch goes back to the very early days of railways, the first proposal being made in 1800. Mr Grace, who lived in Bristol, suggested building a railway between the coal pits and his wharf at Portishead tide mill. It was to be built on a slope so that the descending loaded wagons could draw up the empties. Unfortunately this ingenious plan was not developed.

The next scheme, too, was rather unorthodox. In May 1845, Brunel planned to build a floating pier at Portbury and to connect this with Bristol by an atmospherically worked railway. With this system, like the contemporary one he was installing on the South Devon Railway, no locomotive was needed, but the leading truck would have had a piston attached which fitted into a pipe laid between the rails. When air was withdrawn from this pipe, air pressure would have pushed the piston and the train along. The Portbury Pier and Railway Company obtained its Act the following year, but was wound up in 1851 through lack of funds. This was just as well, for in the event the atmospherically-worked South Devon Railway proved a failure and normal haulage had to be introduced.

The district was determined not to be left off the railway map, so in 1863 the Bristol and Portishead Pier and Railway Company obtained powers to build a line from a junction with the B&ER at Bedminster, to a pier at Portbury. It was intended to run a branch on to Portishead, then only a village, but a change of plan caused the company to abandon the Portbury terminus, and the proposed branch to Portishead became the main line. As was often the case with minor railways, the company did not possess its own locomotives and rolling stock, but was worked by a larger company – in this instance the B&ER.

The amenities of the Ham Green Estate were to be preserved by carrying the railway in two tunnels, but in construction the tunnel east of Ham Green Halt was replaced by a cutting. Altogether there were four tunnels on the branch, making a total length of 1,044 yds.

The 9$^1/_2$ miles of broad gauge single line opened on 18 April 1867 with intermediate stations at Clifton Bridge, Pill and Portbury. Six trains ran on weekdays and one on Sundays, with a journey time from Bristol of forty minutes. Goods traffic was carried by passsenger trains until about July 1875.

The Portishead Railway operated steamer services to Cardiff and Newport (the railway route to South Wales was then via Gloucester as the Severn Tunnel had not been opened), and in summer boats plied to Ilfracombe, with through rail and steamer bookings from the GWR and the Midland Railway.

1871 saw further activity. A Bill was being promoted to make Portishead Pill into a dock. The Avonmouth Company, on the opposite bank, also had plans that year, so both were competing for a subscription of £100,000 from Bristol Corporation. The first ship to enter the dock was the Portishead Company's steamer *Lyn* on 28 June 1879.

The GWR, as successors of the B&ER, bought the railway and pier in 1884, the dock being sold separately. The GWR abandoned the steamer services from Portishead on 1 October 1886, two months before the opening of the Severn tunnel.

The branch was used for an interesting experiment. At that time, the present type of communication cord had not been invented, the first attempt at signalling to the driver being made in 1864: a cord was run from the front guard's van of a passenger train to a large gong mounted on the side of the tender. By 1869 this system had been modified and improved so that the cord extended through rings along the edges of all the coach roofs, and was connected to the emergency whistle on the engine, instead of a gong. This allowed anyone on the train, as long as they were able to lean out of the window and pull the cord, to warn the driver. Then on 23 June 1874 a Bristolian, Reuben Lyon, used the Bristol to Portishead branch to test a further development. It consisted of a bellows and handle fixed to each compartment of a set of three coaches. By pulling down a handle, air was blown from the bellows through a pipe to both the guard's van and the engine, where it sounded whistles inserted into the ends of the pipes. In addition, the handle raised an arm (or a light at night), to indicate the compartment in which the apparatus had been used. This arm was cunningly placed so that it could not be lowered while the train was moving. The pipes doubled as a speaking tube between the front and rear guards, or between a guard and the driver. The inventor tried it with 300 ft of tube, equivalent to ten or twelve coaches, and the six whistles invariably worked. The system was not adopted as it was more expensive to install than a simple cord and did not have any great advantages.

Ashton Gate station had an interesting history. Close to Bristol City Football Ground, it opened on 15 September 1906 for football spectators, and was served by regular trains from 23 May 1926. Following the general withdrawal of the branch's passenger service, it had intermittent use by football specials from 1970 to 1977, and then was reopened temporarily for Dr Billy Graham's 'Mission England' held at the football stadium on 12–19 May 1984. Nearby are the civil engineer's sidings at Ashton Meadows, where bridge and tunnel gauging vehicles are stored.

One of the shortest-lived stations in the country was the picturesquely named and located Nightingale Valley Halt in Clifton Gorge. Opened on 9 July 1928, it was used only in summers until closed on 23 September 1932.

A new passenger station, the first built post-war in Britain, was opened at Portishead on 4 January 1954. Now a garage, it was constructed on a marsh and problems were experienced with subsidence. It was built because the site of the old station was required for part of an enlarged power station.

Branch passenger services were withdrawn on 7 September 1964 and regular freight on 30 March 1981, though occasional Freightliner trains have been worked since that date. The line is retained out of use by BR in the hope that container traffic from Portbury will increase; and additionally there is a chance that the line will be utilized by an Avon Metro scheme.

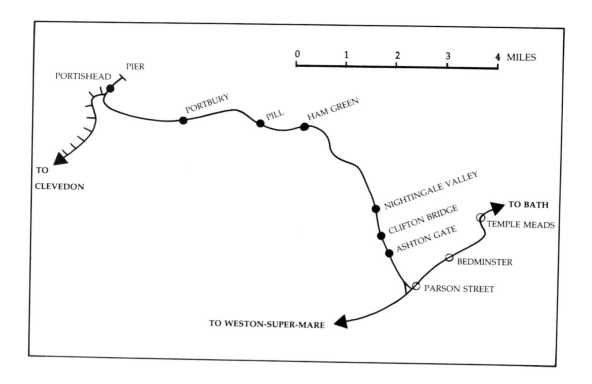

The line west of Clifton Bridge station under construction; view towards Portishead.
c. 1866 Author's Collection

A 'Down' train at Clifton Bridge station hauled by a B&ER 2–2–2WT, (possibly No. 34).
c. 1867 Author's Collection

'Down' railmotor and trailer at Clifton Bridge en route to Portishead. The station has a substantial stone building while, unusually, the platform canopies are of corrugated iron.
c. 1910 Author's Collection

BR Standard Class 3MT No. 82039 arrives at Clifton Bridge with a Bristol to Portishead train. The signalman holds the single line tablet for the fireman to collect. Since the last picture was taken, the platform canopies have had sheets of corrugated iron fixed to their ends. In the distance are Ashton Meadows carriage sidings.

3.3.62 Hugh Ballantyne

Steam railmotor No. 58 arriving at Pill on its way from Portishead to Bristol. The buffers and cylinder head covers have been burnished.

c. 1910 M.J. Tozer Collection

Ex-GWR diesel railcars Nos 25 and 28 near Portbury Shipyard signal box, working the 2.30 p.m. Bristol (Temple Meads) to Portishead.

5.9.58 Author

A BR DMU working the 11.15 a.m. Portishead to Bristol (Temple Meads), leaves the 59 yd long Clifton Bridge No. 1 tunnel. On the right is the fixed distant signal.

7.6.60 R.E. Toop

Weston, Clevedon and Portishead Light Railway

From the GWR at Portishead, a link line led to the Weston, Clevedon and Portishead Light Railway. Although the latter also made a connection with the GWR at Clevedon, the spur there was used very little for exchange as it was so sharply curved. In fact the only sure way to avoid derailment was to inch a wagon round with a pinch bar.

The story of the line started back in 1885, when the necessary Act of Parliament was passed to build the Weston-super-Mare, Clevedon and Portishead Tramway. Termed a tramway, the trains started from a terminus in the middle of the Boulevard at Weston and travelled along it to the outskirts of the town. After that, however, the line continued on its own right of way to Clevedon and Portishead.

Rails were laid for 4 miles out of the 12, but then the company ran out of funds and the lines lay rusting while more cash was raised. At last sufficient was available to reach Clevedon, but then quite a lively quarrel arose between the town council of Weston and the railway.

The track in the Boulevard protruded above the road surface, and the council rightly considered this dangerous. The company was forced to remove it, and this section was never used, so consequently passengers had to walk a mile from the station to the sea – a feature which did not encourage traffic to the line.

Opening to the public on 1 December 1897, the railway quickly got into its stride, special late trains being run just before Christmas in connection with a meat and poultry show at Weston. Preliminary organization had been so slack that the ordered engines had not arrived for the opening, and one had to be borrowed.

The coaches were rather unusual for this country and looked like something from a Wild West film. They were of the American pattern with open verandas at each end; a useful design, as the conductor could pass from one coach to the next collecting fares. These vehicles were obtained quite cheaply as they were the cancelled order of a South American railway. Built of mahogany and made so that they could be packed in cases to be sent abroad, all that was needed to construct them was a single screwdriver and spanner.

Most of the so-called stations did not really exist at all. If a passenger wished to get out, the guard simply waved a red flag, or a lamp at night, as the train approached a level crossing, and the driver carefully pulled up so that the middle verandas of the two-coach train were in the centre of the road. Broadstone had one of the smallest waiting shelters in the country. About the size of a sentry box, it could hold two passengers if they did not object to being in very close proximity.

The coaches were originally lit by paraffin lamps, but the lighting was so weak that the Traffic Manager slung an apparatus under the coaches for generating acetylene gas. The company was then able to claim the honour of being the first railway in Britain to adopt this as a standard lighting system.

There were no lamps on the signals, but an acetylene light on the engine illuminated the track for 150 yds ahead, enabling drivers to see the signals.

In 1899 the company officially became a light railway, and this allowed it to remove most of the level crossing gates. This meant that there was no longer the expense of paying people to open and close them, though admittedly they had done this only in summer. During the winter, the fireman or conductor was supposed to operate the gates, but often a kindly-disposed passer-by obliged.

It was not until August 1907, nearly ten years after the opening of the Weston to Clevedon section, that the railway finally reached Portishead. On this extension, gates protected the dangerous level crossing in front of the GWR's station at Clevedon. Due to rather unusual conditions, these crossing gates could not completely close the roads, and trains had to be preceded by a man carrying two flags – a red to restrain impatient cyclists and pedestrians, and a green to wave on the train.

As traffic on the roads increased, the ungated crossings became dangerous and several accidents occurred. In the 1930s the worst crossings were protected by traffic lights, and an approaching train automatically caused the lights to turn red. Children discovered how it worked, and used to step on the treadle to hold up traffic when there was no train about.

With growing competition from road transport after the First World War, the railway tried to reduce costs in October 1921 by using a petrol-driven railcar carrying thirty passengers. The petrol tank was fitted inside the body and six full petrol cans were kept under the seats, several with missing caps. Eventually someone realized the danger, especially since smoking was allowed, and the tank was fixed in a safer position outside. The engine was inside the car, and when the radiator cap was missing the passengers were able to 'enjoy' a Turkish bath.

In 1934 another Drewry railcar was added to stock. This came second-hand from the Southern Railway, their No. 5, retaining this number on the WCPLR. It seated twenty-six passengers, the luggage compartment taking up about half the body space.

In addition to these two railcars, the WCPLR owned an internal-combustion engined shunter. Purchased in 1921, it was a standard Fordson agricultural tractor fitted with flanged wheels and buffing gear, and ideal for the intermittent requirements of the Wick St Lawrence wharf line. Unfortunately, when being towed from Wick St Lawrence to Clevedon behind a service train, it became derailed and when the guard looked out of his window at Kingston Road, all that remained of the tractor was the engine block. As the shunter had proved its worth, it was replaced in 1926 by another Muir-Hill conversion.

The Wick St Lawrence wharf line was built in about 1913, the WCPLR hoping to develop sea traffic to and from South Wales. It was only suitable for use by ketches, sailing, or motor barges. Traffic was light, a coal vessel calling every few months. Although the WCPLR advertised that 'Seaborne traffic can now be dealt with at Wick St Lawrence' on its timetables and buildings, the wharf was far from being a big success.

Long before the general use by main line companies of concrete sleepers, the WPCLR started manufacturing concrete blocks at Clevedon to replace defective timber sleepers with a more durable material as early as 1919. Unlike those used in contemporary main line company experiments, they proved successful and long-lasting.

The railway went all out to encourage traffic. In 1920 an advertisement tried to persuade industry to develop along the line, pointing out that there were large areas of level land available close to the Bristol and South Wales coalfields. It mentioned that the WPCLR was in direct connection with the trunk lines, that rail and water links with

South Wales were available, and that local taxation was 'reasonable'. 'Manufacturers, especially those desiring to erect works of medium size, are reminded of the fact that it is more advantageous to be in the position of a chief trader on a minor railway system, than a small trader on a trunk line.'

Despite this effort, the WCPLR failed to make a profit after 1909 and a Receiver was appointed. In 1940 a Court Order was made for the Receiver to cease operating the line, which should have been returned to the railway company, but as there were no officers, office, seal or register of books, he could not make this move. The company existed only in name. Since no one had a right to work the line, all traffic was withdrawn after 18 May 1940.

This was not quite the end of the story. The GWR purchased the assets for £10,000 from the Excess Insurance Company, which had bought the right to secure certain sums from the WCPLR. The GWR hoped to use the line to store loaded coal wagons, which had become an embarrassment following the cessation of coal exports after the evacuation of Dunkirk. In the event, the GWR stored very little coal on the line. It scrapped all WCPLR rolling stock and locomotives with the exception of two ex-London, Brighton and South Coast Railway 'Terrier' 0–6–0Ts, which it took into its own stock. Track lifting began in November 1942, and very few traces of the line remain today.

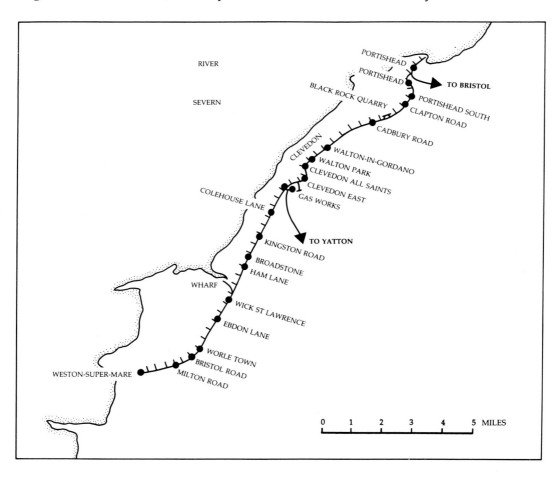

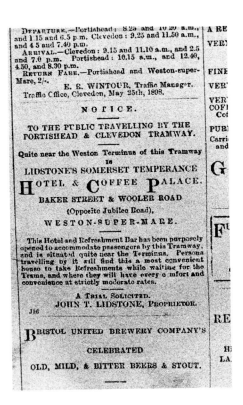

Advert in the *Clevedon Mercury*, 2.7.1898.

WCPLR timetable 12.6.22.

2–2–2WT, later named *Weston*, and derailed coach near Kingston Road. The fence has been temporarily laid flat to give workmen elbow room. On the left is Stephenson 2–4–0T *Portishead*, originally an 0–6–0T.

5.6.1899 G. Rushton Collection

The Weston and Clevedon Light Railway's horse bus which ran between the terminus at Weston-super-Mare and the pier.

c. 1900 Colonel Stephens Railway Museum

A recently installed level crossing cattle grid. The notice reads: 'WC&PT. Trespassers will be prosecuted.'

1899 Author's Collection

Conductor Bill Cullen with cash bag and nippers. Notice that the station platform is only about the height of the rails, and steps have to be mounted in order to enter the carriage.

c. 1909 Author's Collection

Muir Hill tractor No. 1 at Clevedon. This was a standard agricultural Fordson tractor converted using flanged wheels and buffing gear.

c. 1921 E.H. Hazell

View from Clevedon station towards the Triangle. The track is on concrete sleeper blocks made by the WCPLR. The permanent way yard is on the left, and the crossing cabin is on the left just before the gate.

c. 1921 E.H. Hazell

Coal being unloaded at Wick St Lawrence from *Lily*, a 33 ton sailing barge owned by the WCPLR.
c. 1921 W.H. Austen Collection

Broadstone. Notice the unusually small waiting shelter, with a timetable board dated 16 September 1936 in the entrance. Passengers boarded trains from the hard surface of the level crossing. A cattle grid can be seen beyond. The ballast is not quite weed-free, and the telephone poles lean.
Summer 1936 Vaughan Jenkins

0–6–0T No. 2 *Portishead* (an ex-London, Brighton and South Coast Railway engine), arriving at Clevedon with ex-Metropolitan Railway coaches. Notice the large acetylene powered headlamp.

c. 1935 R.W. Kidner

0–6–0ST No. 3 *Weston* at Clevedon is passed by the small Drewry railcar with Guard Jack Riddick on the step.

13.7.35 S.W. Baker

0–6–0ST No. 3 *Weston* crossing the Triangle, Clevedon, with a train to Portishead.

13.7.35 S.W. Baker

WESTON, CLEVEDON & PORTISHEAD RAILWAY.

WESTON-SUPER-MARE
GUY FAWKES CARNIVAL

Torchlight Procession (7.30 p.m.), Fireworks Display, Monster Bonfire, Etc.

PRIZES TO THE VALUE OF OVER £100.

On THURSDAY, Nov. 15th, 1934
CHEAP TICKETS
WILL BE ISSUED TO
WESTON-SUPER-MARE

BY ANY TRAIN; including the Services shown below.

NOTE.—In the event of the Carnival being postponed or abandoned, the special arrangements will be cancelled, and the fares paid for Tickets in advance will be refunded.

Leaving	a.m.	a.m.	p.m.	p.m.	p.m.	p.m.	p.m.	Return Fares 2nd Class s. d.	
CLEVEDON ...	9 50	11 10	2 15	3 55	5 20	6 30	7 30	0	9
COLEHOUSE LANE	9 50	11 10	2 15	3 55	5 20	6 33	7 33	0	9
KINGSTON ROAD ...	9 56	11 16	2 21	4 1	5 26	6 36	7 36	0	9
BROADSTONE ...	9 56	11 16	2 21	4 1	5 26	6 38	7 37	0	9
HAM LANE ...	9 59	11 20	2 24	4 5	5 29	6 39	7 39	0	8
WICK ST. LAWRENCE ...	10 3	11 24	2 28	4 8	5 33	6 43	7 42	0	6
EBDON LANE ...	10 3	11 24	2 28	4 8	5 33	6 46	7 44	0	5
WORLE ...	10 11	11 32	2 36	4 16	5 41	6 50	7 50	0	3
BRISTOL ROAD ...	10 14	11 35	2 39	4 19	5 44	6 53	7 52	0	3

PASSENGERS MAY RETURN BY ANY TRAIN SAME DAY, INCLUDING THE SPECIAL TRAIN.

N.B.—A Special Late Return Train will leave Weston-super-Mare Station at 11.30 p.m. for all Stations to Clevedon.

Children under Three free, over Three and under Fourteen half-fares.
Excursion and other Tickets at fares less than the ordinary fare are issued subject to the Notices and Conditions shewn in the Company's current Time Table.
Tickets are not transferable. Tickets in advance may be obtained at the Booking Stations and usual Offices.

Traffic Office, Clevedon. Nov., 1934. W. H. AUSTEN, Manager

A handbill advertising cheap tickets to Weston-super-Mare for the Guy Fawkes carnival, November 1934.

41

Locomotive No. 4 with the last train, consisting of Cars Nos 2 and 4, arriving at Weston-super-Mare. Notice the passengers carrying gas masks and the gas lamps on the station.

18.5.40 W. Hendry Collection

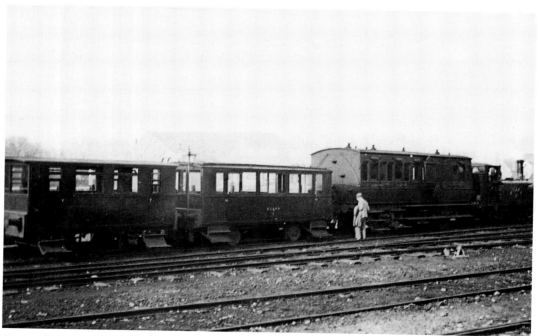

0–6–0T No. 4, and Railcar No. 1 and trailer at Clevedon. The difference in floor and roof heights is most noticeable.

12.3.38 S. Miles Davey, courtesy Peter Davey

Yatton to Clevedon

Almost as soon as the B&ER was opened from Bristol to Bridgwater, someone suggested building a short branch to connect the line with the watering place of Clevedon. As few earthworks were required over the flat moors, the line was constructed quite cheaply. Fences on the branch were set well back from the track so that the line could be doubled if traffic grew sufficiently. Work was completed in July 1847, and the townsfolk celebrated by inviting B&ER directors to a public breakfast. The $3^1/_2$ mile long line made a good start and carried no fewer than 2,000 passengers on the opening day, 28 July 1847.

The branch was worked by the GWR until 1 May 1849 when the B&ER took over. The latter advertised Clevedon rather more than it did Weston-super-Mare, and the volume of traffic was sufficient to justify the provision of a special 560 ft long excursion platform which remained in use until 1879.

The Clevedon branch was converted to standard gauge on Sunday 28 September 1879. About 160 men were split into gangs and started work at midnight on Saturday. By 4 p.m. on Sunday afternoon the track had been narrowed, and was tested by an engine and coach running over the line from Yatton to Clevedon. The usual service was resumed on Monday.

The branch saw interesting motive power. Soon after its opening, it was the scene of the trials of a combined engine and carriage, constructed at Fairfield Works, Bow, in 1848, and named *Fairfield*. Painted sky-blue, it was 40 ft long and had six wheels. The two driving wheels were 4 ft 6 in in diameter, and the remaining wheels were wooden, with a diameter of 3 ft 6 in. The boiler was set vertically and consumed 14.8 lb of coal per mile. It was, in fact, the first workable self-propelled railcar to run a regular passenger service, and the multiple-unit diesel of today can trace its ancestry back to this machine.

Sixty years later, steam railcars again replaced a separate locomotive and coaches. Two cars were stationed at Yatton and one even travelled as far as Swindon each day.

In 1917 passenger trains were worked without a guard, the first section of the GWR to experience this economy. For some years also, Clevedon was without a station-master, the clerk-in-charge acting under the supervision of the station-master at Yatton. Quite understandably the town reacted to this indignity and made its feelings known.

A report issued by the GWR in 1925 gives interesting statistics about the branch. On average four coal and mineral wagons were received daily, in addition to seven goods wagons received and three dispatched. Fifty-three cattle trucks used the branch that year, and 2,000 milk churns were carried.

During the railway strike of 1926, the GWR arranged for the WCPLR's four wheel petrol driven railcar No. 1 and trailer to run a morning and evening peak hour service, but the strike was settled before No. 1 and its crew could use the branch.

Between 1924 and 1936, Clevedon season ticket holders enjoyed a through carriage to and from Bristol. In the evening it was slipped from the main line train at Yatton and worked in by the branch train.

In the 1930s, some of the early GWR diesel railcars used the Clevedon branch at a time when railway diesels were a rare sight indeed. Diesels took over the branch completely in 1960.

In the days of steam, one of the interesting features was the auto train working. The tank engine used to pull the coaches to Clevedon and then, to avoid wasting time uncoupling and running the engine round the train, the locomotive remained at what was now the rear of the train and pushed it to Yatton, the driver moving to a special driving compartment at the end of the coach. Although an engine which was not equipped for auto working should have run round the train at the end of each journey, in practice a blind eye was often turned to this regulation. Although on the return from Clevedon the driver stood in the control vestibule of the auto coach, this was just show, and his fireman on the engine was actually driving.

The interesting account written by a passenger on the 5.15 p.m. Bristol to Clevedon on 10 March 1891 describes the effects of the Great Blizzard of that year.

The journey from Bristol to Yatton was made in fairly good time, but when we got to the latter place, orders to change for Clevedon were given [normally it was a through carriage] and although unusual, were obeyed most readily. Having crossed the line (this by the most direct way to where the Clevedon branch train comes in and leaves), we espied what we found out to be the 4.35 p.m. train from Bristol standing out on the branch line towards Clevedon, in which position it had been for some time. . . . After we had reached the train and were comfortably seated, the guard of the train informed us, with a very complacent smile on his face, that it was no use our expecting to get to Clevedon for some time, as the Clevedon train on its outward journey . . . was blocked; and he signalled to the driver of our train to back into Yatton to allow us to get out and warm ourselves at the waiting room fire. By this time it was after six o'clock.

Seventeen passengers decided that rather than wait for an indefinite period, it would be quicker to walk to Clevedon along the track.

We had not proceeded very far when the kind-hearted and considerate station-master at Yatton despatched a porter to inform us that the train was signalled from Clevedon. . . . A halt was made at the first railway arch, to allow those of us who began to droop to keep their spirits up, by pouring spirits down. . . . About 7.30 p.m. we heard the whistle of a train, which we could not see, and as it might be close upon us, we deemed it advisable for each other's safety to make for the hedge, which was reached after some tumbling about, the snow being between three and four feet deep. As the train did not approach us, we approached the train, and when we got up to what we thought was it, found out it was only the Clevedon engine blocked, the snow having got all round; two or three men with shovels were trying to cut out a passage for it.

The seventeen passengers eventually arrived at Clevedon on foot at about 8.30 p.m.

The passengers who stayed at Yatton were kept waiting until a goods engine, with the snow plough attached, came from Bristol and landed them safely at Clevedon in the small wee hours of the morning. The GWR were so generous that we understand these last-named passengers were not charged excess or any other fare beyond that already paid for in advance by them as season ticket-holders, although the privilege of riding on a goods engine or snow plough is not extended to them.

Being a terminal station, there was always the occasional brake failure when a train failed to stop. One very dramatic incident happened in about 1884, the locomotive itself and two carriages ending in the street outside the station.

Although mixed trains were a feature of the line for some time, goods traffic ceased on 10 June 1963. The branch was closed entirely from 3 October 1966.

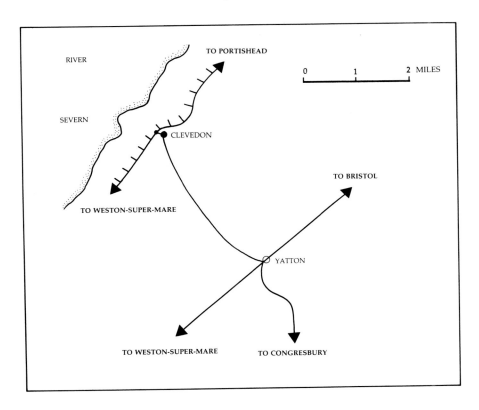

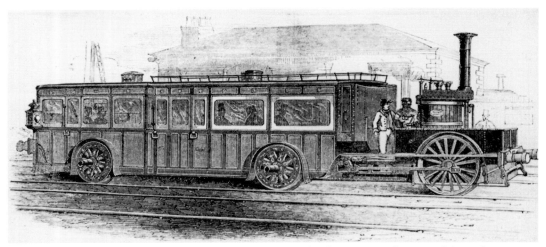

Combined steam engine and coach, No. 29 *Fairfield*. As the floor was within 9in of the rails no steps were required.

c. 1849 *Illustrated London News*

Coaches pushed into the street in a shunting accident at Clevedon. The locomotive can be seen on the left.

c. 1884 Author's Collection

517 class 0–4–2T No. 528 at Clevedon with a train of four four-wheeled coaches. The track is on longitudinal sleepers. The coal wagons have dumb, rather than sprung, buffers. All are from Radstock: that on the far right belongs to Toomer and the other two to Bird & Co.

c. 1898 G. Rushton Collection

517 class 0–4–2T No. 1433 at Clevedon. Displayed on the wall is a Barry Railway timetable and an advertisement for the Walton Park Hotel.

c. 1905 Author's Collection

14XX class 0–4–2T No. 1402 at Yatton with a Clevedon train.

June 1956 W.H. Harbor/Author's Collection

14XX class 0–4–2T No. 1454 near Yatton en route from Clevedon. The leading auto coach is W233, built in 1951. Although similar to the traditional GWR pattern, it was of all-steel construction and had larger windows.

5.6.54 R.E. Toop

Ivatt Class 2MT 2–6–2T No. 41248 near Colehouse Bridge, with a Clevedon Football Club special.
7.8.61 W.H. Harbor/Author's Collection

14XX class 0–4–2T No. 1463 at Clevedon.

25.4.57 Rev. Alan Newman

A single car DMU leaving Clevedon. By the time this photograph was taken the goods sidings had been lifted and the signal box, latterly a ground frame, closed.

c. 1965 D. Payne

Yatton to Cheddar, Wells, Shepton Mallet and Witham

Although the Yatton to Witham line was latterly one branch, it was actually formed by two separate railway companies – the Cheddar Valley Railway and the East Somerset Railway.

The Cheddar Valley line was the outcome of a dispute between the standard gauge Somerset and Dorset Railway and the broad gauge B&ER. The latter proposed building a branch line from Bleadon to Wells, and the S&DR, threatened by this invasion of its territory, retaliated by planning a line from Wells to Yatton with the idea of a future extension to Bristol. A compromise was reached, the B&ER agreeing to abandon its line, and finance and construct the Yatton to Wells branch. The Cheddar Valley and Yatton Railway duly obtained its Act of Parliament in 1864, and another Act the following year transferred the line to the B&ER. The contractors started work in March 1867 and the line was inspected and passed by the Board of Trade inspector, Colonel Yolland, on 30 July 1869.

On the opening day, 3 August 1869, a special train left Bristol at 11 a.m. carrying the B&ER directors. At Axbridge they were greeted by flags, bells and a drum and fife band, while refreshments of cake and champagne were served at Cheddar station, the temporary terminus, which itself was incomplete. The line was opened through to Tucker Street, Wells on the following 5 April.

The Cheddar Valley line was converted to standard gauge in 1875, having the distinction of being the only gauge conversion made by the B&ER. As the branch had been laid with cross-sleepered track, instead of the more usual longitudinal sleepers which the broad gauge party generally favoured, this was a relatively easy operation. Work was begun on Monday 15 November, the directors disapproving of Sunday labour, and the line was ready for reopening on the Thursday.

Winscombe station was a brick building of GWR pattern, and quite a contrast to the substantial B&ER stone structures of the other stations. This was because the original B&ER station was a small, light, timber building like a Swiss chalet, in view of its situation on a newly made embankment. As the district became a residential area, the original building was insufficient, and a new one replaced it in 1905; the ground now having settled, it was built of heavier material. The old station was dragged away on rollers by a traction engine preceded by a man with a red flag, and became the village shop, most of it being removed about 1916. From the opening of the line until 1869, the station was called Woodborough. A nameboard was sent down from Bristol with instructions that it should be set up, and the local carpenter employed for the job spent a laborious afternoon and evening erecting it. For years the old man had successfully concealed the fact that he was illiterate, but the secret was out the next morning when passengers for the first train stared in amazement at the inverted board!

Beyond Winscombe the line rose to Shute Shelf tunnel, 180 yds in length and unlined except at the Yatton end. Ten years after the line was opened, some daring scholars from Sidcot School placed a packet of carefully mixed chemicals on the rails in this tunnel, and the resulting explosion caused the train to pull up abruptly. The culprits were caught and duly lectured on the seriousness of their offence by a representative of the railway. Later the Board accepted a letter of apology from the headmaster and closed the incident.

Shute Shelf was the site of a minor disaster in 1947, when the GWR diesel railcar No. 37 was destroyed by fire.

Cheddar station had an overall roof – unusual for a through branch line station. Another remarkable feature was that it had a refreshment room until 1925. No doubt the prospect of excursion traffic encouraged the directors to provide a more lavish building than at other places.

Before the Milk Marketing Board reorganized the collection of milk, each train had at least one milk van, the solitary Sunday train conveying no less than eight milk vans on the first stage of their journey to London. There was also a large seasonal traffic in strawberries from Lodge Hill, Draycott, Cheddar and Axbridge, three special trains being dispatched each day at the height of the season in addition to all other trains, carrying as much of this traffic as possible. The old varieties of strawberries did not travel well, and it was only with the introduction of Royal Sovereign at the turn of the century that consignments of fruit could be sent by special strawberry train for sale in South Wales, Birmingham, Manchester, Edinburgh and Glasgow. Land was so precious that between Axbridge and Lodge Hill, even the soil between the rails and the boundary fence was cultivated.

There was also quite a considerable tonnage of stone from Sandford and Banwell quarries, which had their own siding and locomotives. The first two engines were purchased from the War Department, one being *Bulford*, from Sir John Jackson Limited's Bulford Camp construction contract in Wiltshire, the other, *Finetta*, coming from the WD line at Codford, also in Wiltshire. From 1949 until rail traffic ceased in September 1964, a vertical boilered Sentinel was used.

The Cheddar Valley line once produced weekly receipts of £20 per mile, and excursion traffic from Bristol to Cheddar and Wells was brisk. With the greater use of roads the line became unprofitable, and was closed to passengers from 9 September 1963. It shut completely from 1 October 1964.

The Cheddar Valley line approached Wells from the west, the East Somerset Railway from the east. The first meeting of the ESR took place on 29 September 1855 at Shepton Mallet when it was planned to build a line from Frome to the town. The Act was granted the following year to build a broad gauge line from Frome to Shepton Mallet, and Wells gave powerful support for an extension to that city. The contractors, Messrs Brotherhood of Chippenham, started work on All Fools' Day 1857, and built the branch in eighteen months, good going considering the heavy clay and cuttings through stone. The line was fenced in for double track, although the cuttings were only wide enough for a single line.

By the autumn of 1857 work had been completed as far as Shepton Mallet, but the Board of Trade inspector could not pass the line as it failed to comply with safety regulations. After the necessary alterations were made, it eventually opened on 9 November 1858 with all the ceremony that Victorians loved on such occasions. 'A prodigious multitude awaited the arrival of the first train with a band of music when *Homer* [a 4–4–0ST built by R. and W. Hawthorn & Co. in August 1854] arrived with the directors, decked with flowers from stem to stern.' (The engine presumably, not the directors!)

Shepton was thrilled that it was no longer reliant on the speed of a horse for connection with the outside world, and the great day ended with a firework display. It is interesting to note that the opening of the ESR brought an end to the Royal Mail coaches from Bath: the last one ran from Bath to Wells via Shepton.

Meanwhile, at a public meeting in Wells, the ESR directors pledged themselves to apply to Parliament for powers to build an extension to Wells on being guaranteed £12,500. A committee was formed to raise this sum, but when an attempted amendment was tried in favour of the Somerset Central Railway, later to become part of the S&DR, the suggestion was greeted with shouts of derision. The extension line Act was granted in 1857 and deviations were sanctioned three years later, this latter Act cancelling a proposed junction with the Somerset Central Railway at Wells, the two lines not joining until sixteen years later.

ESR shares proved unpopular, and difficulties were experienced in raising capital for the extension to Wells. Eventually Messrs Baldwin of London started work late in 1860. Construction took only fourteen months and involved making ten cuttings 50 to 60 ft deep, and building four timber and eight stone bridges.

The first journey over the extension took place on the afternoon of 28 February 1862, when the directors, headed by their chairman, the Marquis of Bath, travelled from Shepton to Wells, where they were greeted by the mayor and council. A procession headed by the Rifle Volunteer Band wended its way from the new terminus to the Swan Hotel for the celebratory meal.

The line opened to the public the following day and brought Bristol half an hour nearer to Wells. The journey was via Westbury and Bath, the Cheddar Valley line not being opened to Wells until 1870.

Four trains ran to Witham daily. Third class passengers were conveyed only by one train, arriving at London six hours and forty minutes after leaving Wells, while first and second class passengers on the same train, who were allowed to catch an earlier connection, arrived at Paddington two hours before them.

The Board of Trade insisted on a turntable being installed at Witham 'otherwise goods traffic would not be sanctioned'. One was dutifully provided, but because the branch only used tank engines initially, it did not function for many years.

The ESR was not a flourishing concern, its income only allowing a dividend to be paid on preference shares, no dividend at all being received by ordinary shareholders. Negotiations took place with the GWR to purchase the undertaking, but these fell through. In January 1874 the ESR received the shattering news that the GWR's Wilts, Somerset and Weymouth line was to be converted from broad to standard gauge, and the GWR invited the ESR to convert too, at an approximate cost of £7,390 – a sum far beyond the slender finances of the company. This forced the ESR's hand and on 2 December 1874 it sold the line to the GWR. As mentioned before, Cheddar Valley trains had arrived at Tucker Street station, Wells, on 5 April 1870, and on 1 January 1878 trains were first run over a connecting link between Tucker Street and the East Somerset station, the latter being relegated to goods traffic.

The ESR station at Wells was a 'light and neat structure' erected by a local builder on the east side of Priory Road opposite the S&DR station. Nearby was an engine shed, turntable and water crane. Shepton Mallet had a busy station and goods yard, while midway a siding served Dulcote Quarry. Blasting operations here were permitted within specified times, but in the interests of safety to passing trains, the actual firing of shots was only allowed when a railwayman had arrived from Wells carrying a 'blasting disc' and the single line staff, thus ensuring that no train could run.

With the development of competing road traffic, the line closed to passengers on 9 September 1963, though the last passenger train from Wells to Witham was an enthusiasts' special in May 1969. Shortly after this, the line was lifted between Wells and Doulting Quarry. The remaining eastern section of the line was brought into more intensive use in June 1970 when Foster Yeoman developed Merehead Quarry. The large, mechanized Merehead Stone Terminal opened in 1971. Initially all rail traffic was moved by BR locomotives, but a second stage saw a new cord line opened on 16 September 1973 to form a triangular junction with the BR line. The company purchased its own locomotives to move stone in the terminal area. In 1984 the third stage was the purchase from the USA of Class 59 engines built by General Motors, to run on BR, and maintained by BR at Merehead. This development has made this part of the ESR still very much a viable commercial proposition.

Meanwhile at Cranmore, David Shepherd formed the Cranmore Railway Company to trade under the name of the East Somerset Railway and preserve locomotives and rolling stock. Early in 1973 an engine shed was built at Cranmore on the site of the old wagon repair shop, which, curiously enough, collapsed in a gale the night before the building of the new shed was to begin!

About 1925 a standard gauge line approximately a mile in length was built on the site of an earlier horse-worked narrow gauge line, running northwards from Cranmore to Waterlip Quarry.

Wanstrow station was paid for by local inhabitants as the railway company was too impecunious to build it. An interesting procedure was carried out at Witham. To release engines from 'Up' trains, the empty passenger vehicles were shunted up the incline towards Wanstrow and then, after the engine had been uncoupled and moved out of the way on to another line, the coaches were allowed to gravitate back into the bay platform.

In the autumn of 1930, the track between Wanstrow and Cranmore was laid on relatively rare steel sleepers, these being some of the first put down by the GWR. When the author saw them in 1957 they were still in good condition.

The Yatton end of the branch had the honour of being used by the royal train. This came about when, in about 1940, King George VI and Queen Elizabeth visited the Bristol Aeroplane Company's works at Filton and the royal train was stabled at Yatton on the Cheddar Valley loop for two nights. Cows were removed from nearby fields so that the royal party would not be disturbed by their lowing at night time. Sawdust was laid to deaden the footsteps of the royal guard.

Bristol to Exeter Railway consignment note, Sandford station, dated 29.6.1874.

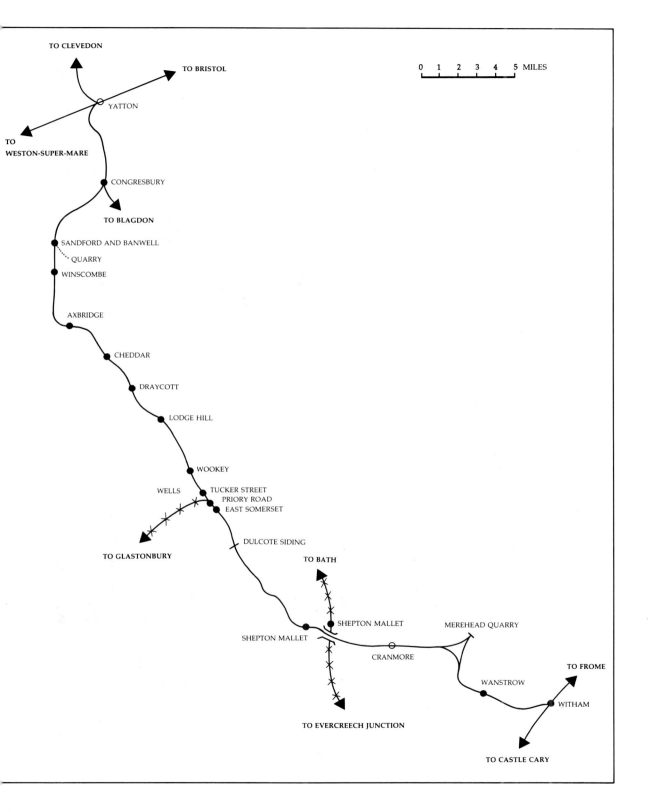

TO CLEVEDON

TO BRISTOL

0 1 2 3 4 5 MILES

YATTON

TO WESTON-SUPER-MARE

CONGRESBURY

TO BLAGDON

SANDFORD AND BANWELL

QUARRY

WINSCOMBE

AXBRIDGE

CHEDDAR

DRAYCOTT

LODGE HILL

WOOKEY

WELLS

TUCKER STREET
PRIORY ROAD
EAST SOMERSET

DULCOTE SIDING

TO GLASTONBURY

TO BATH

SHEPTON MALLET

SHEPTON MALLET

MEREHEAD QUARRY

CRANMORE

TO FROME

WANSTROW

WITHAM

TO EVERCREECH JUNCTION

TO CASTLE CARY

55

Congresbury: Ivatt Class 2MT 2–6–2T No. 41208 heads the 1.27 p.m. Yatton to Wells, while 57XX class 0–6–0PT No. 8746 works an 'Up' goods.

11.3.61 R.E. Toop

The guard flags 8750 class 0–6–0PT No. 3643 away from Axbridge, with the 1.10 p.m. Witham to Yatton.

27.7.63 E. Wilmshurst

View from within Cheddar goods shed: notice the timber platform, the hand crane chain, and loading gauge to check that no lineside structures will be fouled.
May 1965. W.H. Harbor/Author's Collection

Cheddar train shed was deteriorating rapidly. The end windows have been removed and the cross beam supported. The engine is North British diesel-hydraulic Type 2 D6342 heading the 10.49 a.m. Saturdays-only Witham to Yatton.

17.8.63 Hugh Ballantyne

2201 class 0–6–0 No. 2206 snowed up near Draycott.

December 1962 Author's Collection

8750 class 0–6–0PT No. 3795 approaching Wells (Tucker Street), with the 11.12 a.m. Saturdays-only Yatton to Witham. The distant arm below the home signal is a fixed distant signal arm. To the right are cattle pens – a feature of many country stations – and a stone goods shed of considerable size.

28.5.60 R.E. Toop

A pair of single ended ex-GWR diesel railcars with intermediate trailer at Wells (Tucker Street), working a Yatton to Witham train. The porter wears bicycle clips. Does he intend to make a quick getaway off duty after the train's departure?

c. 1955 M.E.J. Deane

An 0–6–0PT hauls a weed-killing train made from old tenders near East Somerset signal box, Wells.

Author's Collection

An hotel horse bus waits outside the 'Up' platform of Shepton Mallet station.

c. 1900 Author's Collection

Beyer Peacock Type 3 diesel-hydraulic D7022 crosses the Somerset and Dorset line at Shepton Mallet with a ballast train.

17.2.65 P. Strong

Foster Yeoman No. 22 *Merehead*, an ex-BR 08 class, at Torr Works.

31.5.78 Author

Delivery day at Merehead for the General Motors locomotives. The four Class 59 engines were hauled from Southampton to Westbury by a Class 47 and then taken in separate pairs to Merehead. This picture shows the second pair just arrived from Westbury. Notice the General Motors switcher, built to the United States loading gauge and not used on BR tracks, towering above the large main line locomotives.

24.1.86 Hugh Ballantyne

Congresbury to Blagdon

The history of this fascinating line started in November 1881, when the Radstock, Wrington and Congresbury Junction Railway was promoted. This was to be a line fourteen and three quarter miles in length running from Farrington Gurney, on the Bristol and North Somerset Railway, to Congresbury. Its objects were to serve an agricultural population of 20,000 and develop the large coal and iron fields believed to be on each side of the River Yeo. When the bill came before the Select Committee of the House of Commons in April 1882, there was little opposition. The GWR had faith in the proposed line and promised to work it for a half share of the profits. Its engineer, Price Williams, estimated building costs at £2,300 a mile, an exceptionally low figure since the Cheddar Valley line had cost £12,000 a mile, and that from London Bridge to Charing Cross line no less than £1,000 per yard.

The Radstock, Wrington and Congresbury Junction Railway bill received its Act of Parliament in 1882, but unfortunately the shares were not all taken up and an Act of Abandonment was passed four years later.

The idea was not completely shelved, however, and ten years later a less ambitious plan was produced – a light railway from Congresbury to Blagdon with a short branch running to the waterworks there. This latter line could claim the rare distinction of being a branch of a branch of a branch. The course of the new line was almost identical to that of the 1882 plan.

In November 1896 an application was made for a Light Railway Order. The statutory inquiry was held at Wrington on 20 May 1897, where no objections were raised, and the line had the support of the Bristol Waterworks. This latter company was just about to build a reservoir at Blagdon and a railway would prove invaluable for bringing machinery and materials to the site. The GWR offered to finance, construct and work the line if an Order were granted. The Light Railway Order was confirmed on 18 March 1898, and shortly afterwards the contractor started work.

His initial task was relatively easy, for the stretch from Congresbury as far as Wrington required few earthworks, but for the section beyond some substantial excavation was needed.

When at last the line was finished, the railway was fully aware of the value of newspaper publicity and invited the press to a preview of the line on 25 November 1901, before its public opening on 4 December. On this latter date, all the local industries closed in order that their employees could celebrate the occasion. Bristol Waterworks opened the grounds of Blagdon Reservoir to the public, while Baron Winterstoke, champion of the line, entertained local dignitaries at Coombe Lodge after they had ridden over the new railway. Altogether 1,500 passengers were carried on the opening day. The first engine to work the branch was 2–4–0T No. 1384, which had been built in 1875 for the Watlington and Princes Risborough Railway. There was no engine shed at Blagdon, so a tarpaulin was thrown over her at night. Later she was bought by the Weston, Clevedon and Portishead Light Railway and named by them *Hesperus*. She ended her career rather ignominiously when a wooden bridge at Wick St Lawrence collapsed under her weight.

Most of the land adjacent to the line was used for dairy farming and the railway was invaluable for transporting milk, butter and cheese to market in the days before rapid road travel. The four passenger trains which ran daily each way were allowed thirty minutes for the eight mile run from Yatton to Blagdon, necessitating only one change for main line passengers. The Clevedon branch steam railmotor made a single trip daily and sometimes ran out of steam on the gradient between Wrington and Blagdon. All trains were subject to a limit of 25 mph.

In 1904, day trips were run from Bristol stations to view Blagdon reservoir and Burrington Combe. The journey to Langford was by rail, and from there charabancs took tourists over the Mendip Hills to Cheddar from where they returned by rail to Bristol.

One of the longest and most gruesome passenger trains on the branch ran on 3 March 1914, carrying the body of Colonel Llewellyn of Langford Court, a director of the GWR and also of Bristol Waterworks. He died in Devon and his cadaver was brought back to Burrington for the funeral. It left Topsham at the Exmouth branch, at 11.09 a.m. in a brake composite, which was transferred at Exeter St David's to the 11.02 a.m. from Paignton which made a special stop at Yatton for it to be uncoupled. Meanwhile a special train left Bristol Temple Meads at 1.50 p.m. consisting of two brake composites and the directors' saloon. This left Yatton at 2.15 p.m. for Blagdon, composed of the Wrington branch engine, the Bristol engine, the Bristol coaches, directors' saloon, coach with the body, and the Wrington branch train bringing up the rear. As the special funeral train was combined with the regular 2.15 p.m. to Blagdon, it was arranged that the lengthy train would stop at all stations with just the branch carriages at the relatively short platforms, but at Burrington it would stop with the special carriages at the platform, later drawing forward for local passengers to alight. On arrival at Blagdon, the coaches were shunted ready for the 3.55 p.m. return special. Both engines worked the normal 3.05 p.m. to Yatton, and on arrival at Congresbury the Bristol engine was detached and returned to Blagdon to work the 3.55 p.m. special.

When local bus services were introduced they siphoned off most of the passengers, causing the line to be closed to this traffic on 14 September 1931, it being one of the first branches to suffer such a withdrawal. Goods trains still continued running to Blagdon, but on 1 November 1950 Langford, Burrington and Blagdon stations were closed to goods traffic, the rails being lifted early in 1952. Wrington was closed to goods on 10 June 1963 and the remainder of the branch was lifted the following year.

One of the more unusual features of the line was its ungated level crossings. Cattle grids prevented animals straying on the railway and vehicles were warned by three notices: 'Beware of Trains'; 'Crossing No Gates'; and 'Trains Cross Here'. Beside the track approaching the crossings was a 10 mph limit sign for trains, and nearer the crossing a board marked 'SW' (Sound Whistle). Gates were provided for the level crossing at Wrington, and also at Langford where the branch crossed the busy Bridgwater road. Between Congresbury and Wrington the line had no embankments or cuttings, and had a switchback appearance as it followed the lie of the land.

The original rails lasted throughout the life of the branch and were flat-bottomed and spiked directly to the sleepers. One spike was knocked in on each side of the rail, but alternate sleepers had one spike on the outside only. On the 1 in 50 gradient between Langford and Burrington, ordinary bull-head chaired track was used to prevent rail-creep on the slope.

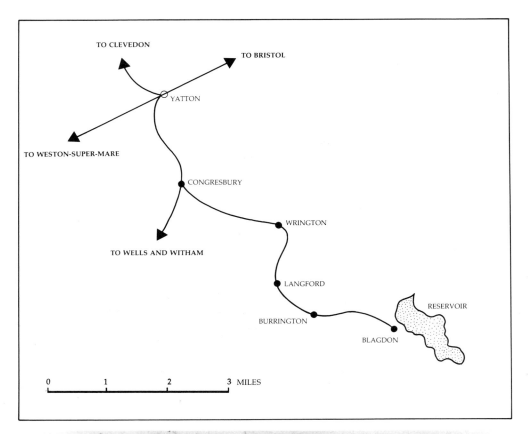

TO CLEVEDON

TO BRISTOL

YATTON

TO WESTON-SUPER-MARE

CONGRESBURY

WRINGTON

TO WELLS AND WITHAM

LANGFORD

RESERVOIR

BURRINGTON

BLAGDON

0   1   2   3 MILES

The simple station building has an integral roof and canopy. Beyond is a cast iron gents urinal and a corrugated iron oil hut. In the distance is the goods yard with coal wagons predominant. Left of the station sign is the weighbridge, carrying advertisements for 'Barber Bros Coal & Coke Merchants. Depot for Bricks, Tiles, Pipes and Sanitary Goods.' Notice the typical light railway flat-bottomed track.

c. 1910 Author's Collection

58XX class 0–4–2T No. 5813 at Wrington. To the right is a hand crane for loading and unloading heavy goods from wagons. The brake van bears the legend 'Yatton RU', the 'RU' standing for 'Restricted Use'.

27.8.54 Author

Track and cattle grid at the ungated Stock Lane crossing. The flat-bottomed track shows up well in this picture.

27.8.54 Author

A party from the Camp Coach at Blagdon. On the left is Bert Maslin; William Cockram, station-master, is seated; Driver George Van Klaveran is on the right.

c. 1937 Author's Collection

Blagdon, terminus of the Wrington Vale Light Railway. The multitude of wagons probably belonged to the contractor who built the line.

c. 1901 Author's Collection

The last passenger train about to leave Blagdon. Notice the low platform.

12.9.31 Author's Collection.

The 'Blagdon, Wrington & Yatton Express' – a comic card postmarked 21 March 1917. Similar cards were published for other branch lines.

Author's Collection

Weston-super-Mare Branch and Loop

The Bristol and Exeter Railway took a direct route between Bristol and Bridgwater. Of necessity it had to curve round the western end of the Mendip Hills, but its main line did not call at Portishead, Clevedon and Weston-super-Mare, these being served by branches. The Weston-super-Mare branch ran $1^1/_2$ miles from Weston junction, the present loop line not being opened until 1884. Weston junction station was situated approximately midway between the later Worle and Uphill junctions.

With the opening of the branch on 14 June 1841, trains on the single track were drawn by horses between Weston junction and Weston-super-Mare, passenger trains generally consisting of three four-wheeled coaches drawn by three horses in tandem fashion ridden by boys, various accidents occurring to both animals and their riders. In 1847, 'as the last train was proceeding along the branch line from Weston to the junction of the Great Western Railway to meet the two o'clock Down train and the half past five Up train, at a quarter of a mile from the station, one of the horses, suffering from a diseased heart, fell upon the rails and the carriages passed over it causing immediate death. The train was thrown off the line and the passengers finished the journey on foot.' This was one of several incidents of horses being killed and their riders injured. When the horses had to pull against the wind, the $1^1/_2$ mile journey took half an hour and many passengers preferred to walk down the line as it was quicker.

As a consequence of a memorial presented to the railway in October 1847, from the beginning of 1848 a steam-hauled express was worked from Weston-super-Mare to Bristol in the morning, with a corresponding 'Down' train in the evening. Except for these two trains, the rest were worked by horses, and thus for three and a quarter years, steam and animal traction were in use at the same time. The horses for the branch were provided by the GWR until the expiration of that company's lease on 30 April 1849, when the B&ER operated its own system. Around 1850, *Fairfield*, the early steam railcar described in the Clevedon section, worked the branch.

From 1 April 1851 all the branch trains were worked by locomotives. In later years mails for Weston-super-Mare, dropped by the 8.10 p.m. from Paddington, were worked in from Weston Junction at 1.10 a.m. by 'Post Office Trolley'. Nothing seems to be known about this vehicle or its motive power. Certainly the GWR service timetables for October 1886 (after the opening of the standard gauge only loop line), mention that the 'Trolley' worked over the old Weston branch line from a point near the gas works sidings to a siding at the old Weston junction. This was for the purpose of carrying Weston-super-Mare mail bags to and from the 'Up' and 'Down' broad gauge night mails. A mail exchange apparatus was situated at the junction, allowing mail bags to be dropped and picked up without the main line train having to stop.

The history of stations at Weston-super-Mare is quite involved. The original terminus was in Alexandra Parade near the present floral clock; then on 20 July 1866 the branch was doubled and cut back to a large new train shed-style terminus in Locking Road, designed by Francis Fox, the B&ER's engineer. The broad gauge branch had a third rail added on 1 July 1875 to accommodate standard gauge rolling stock, and four years later broad gauge trains were completely withdrawn from the branch.

To ease working by enabling through trains to call, a standard gauge Weston-super-Mare loop was opened on 1 March 1884, leaving the main line at Worle junction, passing through Weston and regaining the main line at Uphill junction. This loop superseded the old branch from Weston junction, which was closed to passenger traffic together with the junction station. This caused all main line trains to be formed of standard gauge stock in order to call at the new Weston station, also designed by Francis Fox, on the loop, the terminal station at Weston being relegated to the goods department.

To cope with the growing number of holiday-makers, an excursion platform had been opened at Locking Road in 1866. Enlarged to four platforms on 8 April 1914, it was chiefly used in the summer months, finally closing on 6 September 1964. In its heyday, on a Bank Holiday Monday the GWR and LMS (the latter's engines worked through to Weston-super-Mare) brought in excess of 30,000 passengers in thirty special trains, and the normal two-road station could not have coped with such numbers.

Worle station, close to the junction, opened with the new loop line on 1 March 1884 and closed on 2 January 1922, the buildings remaining until their demolition in the mid-sixties. Weston Milton Halt opened on 3 July 1933, being refurbished and having a new car park constructed jointly by BR and Avon County Council, in 1983.

In the interests of rationalization, although Weston-super-Mare station itself retained double track serving the two through platforms, the rest was made single beyond the station to Uphill junction on 12 October 1969, and to Worle junction on 31 January 1972. The disused platform at Weston Milton was removed to the new Lympstone Commando station on the Exmouth branch.

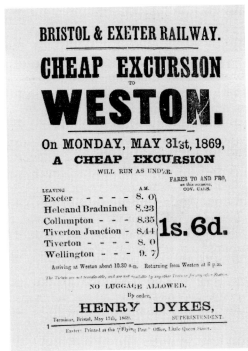

Handbill: B&ER cheap day excursion to Weston-super-Mare, dated 17 May 1869.

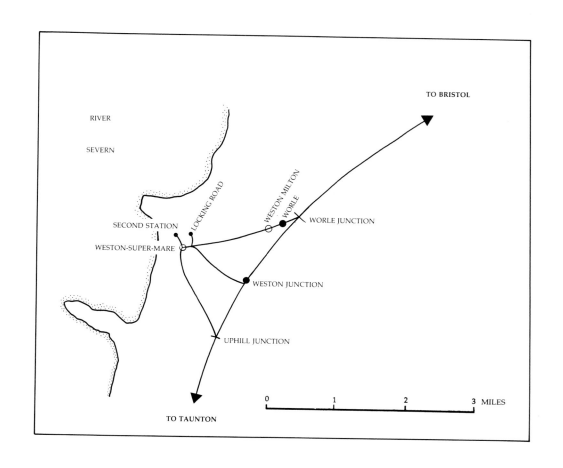

RIVER SEVERN

TO BRISTOL

LOCKING ROAD

WESTON MILTON

WORLE

SECOND STATION

WORLE JUNCTION

WESTON-SUPER-MARE

WESTON JUNCTION

UPHILL JUNCTION

TO TAUNTON

0   1   2   3 MILES

A sketch made in 1846 depicting the original Weston-super-Mare station, and a train drawn by horses.

Author's Collection

The 1884 Weston-super-Mare station view 'Up'. Notice the very attractive gas lamp, the delightful platform canopy and valance, and also the windshields to protect waiting passengers from draughts caused by westerly winds.

c. 1910 M.J. Tozer Collection

Atbara class 4–4–0 No. 3407 *Malta* with an 'Up' train at Weston-super-Mare. This engine was converted to the 'City' class in November 1908.

April 1906 M.J. Tozer Collection

View from the 'Up' end of Weston-super-Mare station. An 0–6–0 is shunting empty carriages on the centre road, while a tank engine heads a train for Bristol from the 'Up' main platform. Another stands in the 'Up' bay. Notice the wide 'Down' platform to give plenty of room for holiday-makers and day trippers to circulate.

c. 1905 Lens of Sutton

4–4–0 No. 3818 *County of Radnor* heads a train that has just arrived at Platform Two, Locking Road station, Weston-super-Mare.

c. 1924. Author's Collection

Preserved 4–4–0 No. 3440 *City of Truro* at Locking Road with Westward TV Exhibition Train.
4.3.61 R.E. Toop

Peak class D147 leaves Locking Road station with the 12.15 p.m. to Sheffield. A Hymek diesel-hydraulic stands at another platform, while a steam engine has just been turned on the table, to the right.

27.7.63 E. Wilmshurst

The broad gauge 'Down' 'Cornishman' passes Uphill Junction signal box, while a train from the Weston-super-Mare branch waits for it to pass. Notice the mixed gauge track on the main line, with narrow only on the branch. On the box hang plates indicating the state of the equipment in the box. The round signalling plate has an 'S' and telegraph a diamond with 'T'. If in working order the plates showed white letters on a black ground. In the event of a fault, a plate was reversed, showing a red letter on a white ground. These plates could be seen from passing trains by linesmen or inspector. In this view both sets of equipment need attention. Observe the signal-man giving a hand signal with a flag.

4.9.1891 Rev. A.H. Malan

No. 5902 *Howick Hall* derailed at Worle Junction. It was hauling a train on the main line and collided with a train from Weston-super-Mare.

Author's Collection

Dunball Wharf and Bridgwater Docks

The history of the 792 yd long branch to Dunball wharf started in May 1836, when the Bristol and Exeter Railway was mooted and an Act authorized a branch from the main line to Dunball wharf. However, the company spent all its money on constructing the main line and had none left with which to build the branch, yet the need for such a line was still felt. So, in 1844, the B&ER directors laid a private horse-worked tramway from the main line to the wharf, principally used for coal traffic.

This tramway speeded fuel deliveries to Taunton and the West, as at this date there was no through rail communication between South Wales and the West of England for until the Severn tunnel was opened in 1886, rail traffic had to travel via Gloucester. The opening of this tramway meant that coal could be shipped from South Wales and the Forest of Dean to Dunball, and then distributed onwards by rail. In fact, some ship owners diverted their craft from Bridgwater Docks, then without rail communication, to Dunball wharf. This meant that the railway was now competing for coal traffic with the Bridgwater and Taunton Canal and the Grand Western Canal. Consumers benefited as the cost of rail transport for coal from Dunball to Tiverton fell from 4s. 9d. a ton in 1851, to 1s. 3d. a ton the following year.

In 1867 the B&ER was authorized by an Act of Parliament to buy and extend Dunball wharf and convert the horse tramway into a locomotive-worked branch. Rebuilding complete, the first steam-hauled train ran over the mixed gauge branch in November 1869. The extension of Dunball wharf itself was finished in 1874. Between 1876 and 1881 the Wharf dealt with about 100,000 tons of traffic annually, but after this quantities declined, especially following the opening of the Severn tunnel in 1886 when so much of the South Wales trade, formerly by sea, was transferred to rail. Nevertheless, a daily coal train still ran from Dunball to Exeter, and remained broad gauge until final conversion in May 1892.

In more recent years the wharf dealt with timber, sand, gravel, cement and molasses. There were also J. Bibby's animal feedstuffs distribution depot and an Esso petroleum depot to offload supplies brought by barge across the channel from the Milford Haven refinery.

Speed over the branch was restricted to 5 mph and special regulations were in force for crossing the A38: a man with a red flag was required to bring road traffic to a halt and loads were limited to a maximum of twenty-five wagons when the engine was propelling its train. A weighbridge was provided for ascertaining the weight of the railway wagons and their contents.

The short but busy branch line was only capable of taking the smallest GWR shunting engines, either a four-wheeler, or a very light six-coupled one, and this was stabled at Bridgwater. One of the interesting engines which worked the branch was 0–6–0ST No. 2194 *Kidwelly*, inherited by the GWR when it took over the Burry Port and Gwendraeth

Valley Railway in South Wales. Another locomotive seen on the line was No. 1338, built by the Cardiff Railway and the only one from this company to stray so far from home under GWR ownership. It could proudly claim that, when withdrawn in September 1963, it was the last Cardiff Railway engine remaining in British Railways' service. The Dunball wharf branch itself closed on 19 March 1962.

When the B&ER was opened, Bridgwater Corporation joined the wharf on the River Parrett to the main line by means of a horse tramway called the Communication Works. Opened in 1845, it was leased to the B&ER in 1859 and purchased by them four years later. In 1865 Bridgwater Town Council considered an application from the B&ER to extend the tramway across the Parrett to the docks and cattle market. The council rejected the idea, objecting to navigation being interrupted. The following year a public meeting on 10 February unanimously approved of the B&ER purchasing the Bridgwater and Taunton Canal, and extending the railway by means of a telescopic span to the docks. At the same time, standard gauge was added to the existing broad gauge and the horse tramway converted to locomotive operation. Although the broad gauge was abolished in May 1892, mixed gauge track still existed in a coal merchant's yard fifty years later.

Completed in January 1871, the telescopic bridge, a rare but not unique type, took about fifteen months to build at a cost of £8,000. Messrs Warburton Brothers, Bristol, erected the masonry, Lloyds, Foster & Co. of Wednesbury supplying the wrought ironwork. Officially opened in March 1871, for the first eight months of its life it was worked by manual winches at each end, but then a stationary steam engine was installed in a brick cabin on the east bank.

The bridge was divided into three sections and this sequence was followed to open it. The signals at each end of the bridge were placed at danger and a steel arm locked across the rails, physically preventing trains from trying to pass and falling into the river. Gates across the footbridge and rail track were locked. Safety precautions having been taken, the bridge's stationary steam engine was started and the gears engaged to move the traversing section sideways on special rails across to its pit. The gears were then changed to drive the chain drum in order to move the rolling main section, spanning most of the river, back lengthways into the space vacated by the first section. The third section of the bridge remained fixed.

There was an exciting moment in 1913 when the stationary engine broke down. As it was imperative that the span across the river be opened, gangers pulled the bridge open with ropes.

It is believed that the bridge was not opened after 1953, because the upper berths on the river fell out of use. With shipping decreasing as the winding narrow estuary of the River Parrett was unsuited to modern vessels, the docks branch closed in April 1967, the docks themselves officially closing on 31 July 1971.

Shunting duties in Bridgwater Docks were undertaken by small tank engines, such as 1361 class 0–6–0ST No. 1362 in the post-Second World War years, but was also the haunt of an early internal-combustion petrol shunting locomotive. This was a four-wheeled Simplex from the Motor Rail & Tram Company. Built in 1923, it operated at Bridgwater from 1932 until 1939. No. 15 carried a standard GWR number plate, but No. 23, a similar machine also used at the Docks and built in 1925, had its number merely painted on. No. 15 had completely open sides to its cab, while No. 23 had partly-sheeted sides with two cab doors on each side of the body. At each end were sliding windows. No. 23 carried an auto coach-type warning gong. These shunters were ideal for intermittent work required on the Dock sidings and their 5 ft 6³/₄ in wheelbase made them very suitable for working sharply-curved sidings. Both machines weighed 8 tons and were equipped with four-cylinder engines developing 40 bhp at 1000 rpm. Chain drive was provided to both axles through a ten-speed gear-box. No. 15 was cut up in 1951 and No. 23 in 1960.

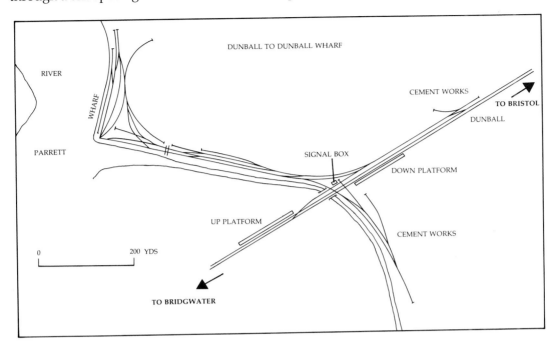

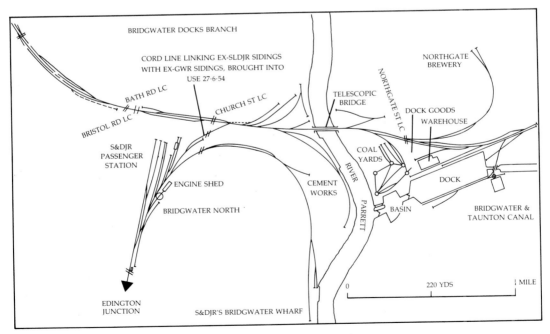

Dunball, view 'Down'. The ground frame hut is on the left, and the siding to the wharf on the right.

c. 1895 Author's Collection

Dunball, view 'Up'. Notice the staggered platforms and a dog with a letter in its mouth. The timber platform is gritted, probably to prevent passengers slipping in wet weather. The line to the wharf led off to the left of the signal box.

c. 1906 Author's Collection

View 'Down' at Dunball showing the wharf branch curving off. On the photographer's side of the signal box a line from a cement works is given access to the GWR via a wagon turntable.
c. 1906. M.J. Tozer Collection

0–6–0ST No. 2194 *Kidwelly*, ex-Burry Port and Gwendraeth Valley Railway, shunting at Dunball Wharf. A vessel is tied to the bollard.

3.3.45 Pursey Short

1361 class 0–6–0ST No. 1362 shunting at Dunball Wharf.

c. 1952 C.B. Cann/P.Q. Treloar Collection

Bridgwater, view north. In this view coal wagons have been derailed on the crossover. The docks branch curves left away from the main line.

c. 1935 Author's Collection

Retracting bridge over the River Parrett. The machinery in the engine house, right, moves the section of rail in the foreground to the right, leaving a space into which the span beyond can be retracted.

8.10.66 Author

The pit into which the span is slid.

8.10.66 Author

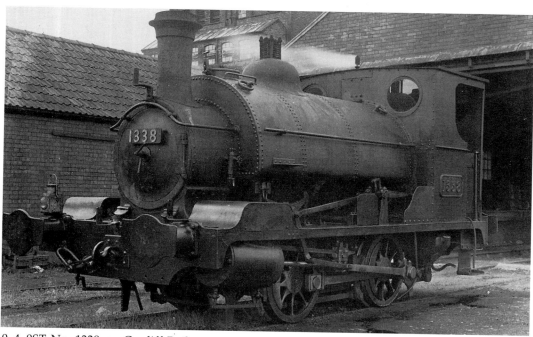

0–4–0ST No. 1338, ex-Cardiff Railway now preserved at Didcot Railway Centre, at Bridgwater shed. This locomotive was used on the docks branch. Notice the unusually shaped buffers.

R.J. Buckley

0–4–0 petrol locomotive No. 15, built in 1923 and used on the dock branch.
February 1951 Author's Collection

204 bhp diesel shunter D2140 at Bridgwater Docks. Notice the radiator blind to keep the engine warm.

18.1.65 P. Strong

Durston to Athelney, and Langport to Yeovil

In its latter years, the $2^1/_4$ miles of single track from Athelney through Lyng Halt to Durston looked like a superfluous oddity, as it was paralleled by the Castle Cary to Taunton main line. It was railway history which caused such a curious situation.

Back in the summer of 1844 the B&ER planned to build a branch from Durston to Weymouth, but in the autumn it had second thoughts and decided to terminate at Yeovil. In 1849 the broad gauge branch was completed from Durston to Martock, but lay rusting until the remainder of the line to Hendford, on the outskirts of Yeovil, was finished. The delay was caused by a shortage of funds, the company already having heavy financial commitments elsewhere. Works on the single line branch resumed in 1852, and it was finally opened to passenger traffic on 1 October 1853, and to goods on 26 October. On 2 February 1857 trains ran through to the Wilts, Somerset and Weymouth Railway station at Yeovil, Pen Mill.

When the standard gauge Salisbury and Yeovil Railway (later part of the London and South Western Railway) was opened on 1 June 1860, trains on this line terminated at the B&ER's Hendford station until Yeovil Town Joint station opened on 1 June 1861, the terminus at Hendford then being relegated to the goods department.

Yeovil Town Joint station, built in Tudor style, had a central waiting room flanked by two Ladies' rooms, on each side of which were the booking offices and houses of the respective station-masters – each company providing its own. There were also no less than four signal boxes: the B&ER and the London and South Western Railway both had one at each end of the station, while the platform staff were of no less than three types – Joint, B&ER and LSWR. The two platforms were spanned by roofs with longitudinal skylights containing about 15,000 sq ft of glass. All the lines and sidings were of mixed gauge.

Friction occurred between the standard and broad gauge factions when, in 1867, the standard gauge Somerset and Dorset Railway planned to construct a branch to Bridgwater. This would have been in direct competition with the broad gauge B&ER so, in order to give standard gauge communication between Yeovil and Bridgwater as an alternative to the proposed LSWR and S&DR lines, the B&ER was forced to pay £125,000 and lay a third rail from Highbridge, where it made a junction with the S&DR, through Bridgwater and Durston to Yeovil.

On 30 June 1879 the mixed gauge branch was completely converted to standard gauge and with it went the nuisance and expense of transhipping goods at Hendford between wagons of the two gauges. The LSWR, no longer needing its independent line from the Town station to Hendford, reduced it to a siding.

In 1876 the branch became GWR property when the B&ER was amalgamated with the GWR. Towards the end of the nineteenth century, critics of the GWR claimed that the company's initials stood for 'Great Way Round'. To a certain extent this was true, and the GWR decided to shorten its line to the West. The new route from Reading to Taunton via Westbury used existing lines for part of the way, though their alignment was improved to main line standards, but between Castle Cary and Curry Rivel a completely new line had to be laid.

For the four miles from Curry Rivel to Athelney, the new line followed the old B&ER's Yeovil branch, which was raised above flood level and made into a double track route. An entirely new line was built from Athelney to Cogload Junction, bypassing Lyng Halt and Durston junction. This explains why the single track to Lyng Halt existed: until its history is known it seems quite superfluous.

At last the new line was ready and this shortened line to the West had to be opened on 1 July 1906, a day early, after a section of Box tunnel fell in, blocking the line used by the West of England expresses.

To combat road competition, the GWR opened unstaffed stations: Thorney and Kingsbury Halt on 28 November 1927, and Lyng Halt on 24 November 1928, while Hendford Halt followed on 2 May 1932. Speed over the branch was restricted to 55 mph.

In 1936 a non-stop diesel railcar service was introduced over the branch on Mondays to Fridays. In the forward direction the service originated at Weymouth, affording a unique through working, while the return timing continued semi-fast to Trowbridge and stations thence to Bristol. The Yeovil to Taunton express timings showed a saving of about twenty minutes on steam stopping trains, despite the necessity to stop to exchange the single line staff.

During the Second World War, to keep SR Exmouth junction crews familiar with an alternative route, they worked, on an SR T9 class 4–4–0, (often Nos 709, 721 or 724), the 10.15 a.m. Exeter St David's to Taunton and the 2.05 p.m. Taunton to Yeovil, returning with the 4.50 p.m. Yeovil to Taunton and the 6.20 p.m. Taunton to Exeter. The T9s primed if Yeovil water was used, so they did not take water there, but with their large capacity tender tanks there was no water shortage problem.

Around Langport station and from Athelney to Lyng the line was liable to flooding, and on one such occasion in November 1873 a newspaper reported that 'When the wind was rough, waves beat against the carriages.'

Messrs Petters, which made stationary oil engines and also traded as Westland Aircraft Ltd, had their own private siding at Hendford (a mile from Yeovil Town), opened in August 1913 and closed in September 1965, aircraft parts being dispatched by rail. Petter and Westland workers used the adjacent Hendford Halt, opened 2 May 1932. All types of Westland aircraft began with a 'W', such as Wapity, Whirlwind and Wyvern, the exception being Lysander. This was because the Hawker Hector was the first Army co-operation aircraft and the next, built by Westlands, had to be named Lysander.

With the development of road traffic, the branch became uneconomic to operate and was closed to passenger traffic between Durston and Athelney, and Curry Rivel junction and Hendford, on 15 June 1964, and closed completely on 6 July the same year, the track being lifted in October 1965. Yeovil Hendford to Pen Mill was closed on 6 May 1968. Platform components from Montacute were used to build Doniford Bridge Halt on the preserved West Somerset Railway.

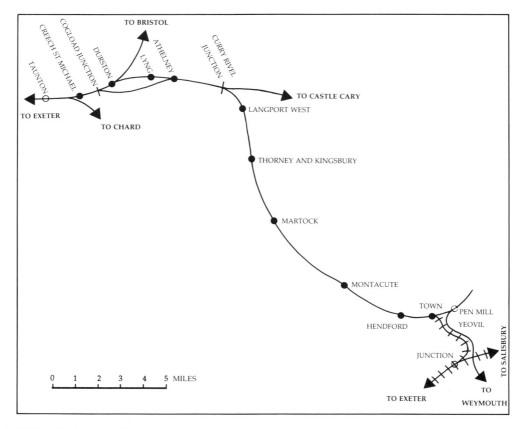

8750 class 0–6–0PT No. 3733 at Durston working the 12.38 p.m. Saturdays-only Yeovil to Taunton. The Taunton to Bristol main line is on the left.

2.6.62 R.E. Toop

D2141 with a freight from the Yeovil branch joins the 'Down' main line at Durston. At the 'Up' platform is a DMU working the 12.30 p.m. Saturdays-only Taunton to Bristol (Temple Meads).

2.6.62 R.E. Toop

Langport West station, view 'Up'. Sheeted wagons stand in the goods yard to the left of the station building. The platform in the foreground is unusually wide for a branch line station. Beyond the passenger station, part of the goods shed can be seen. The passenger train consists of a varied selection of vehicles: two bogie clerestories, a six-wheeler, four-wheeler, and four-wheeled guard's van.

c. 1906 Author's Collection.

Taunton to Yeovil passenger train entering the flooded Langport West station.

c. 1911 Author's Collection

Floods at Langport West: the signal box and goods shed. The signal box has 'S' and 'T' plates hanging beyond the further window.

November 1894 Author's Collection

Standard Goods class 0–6–0 No. 511 at Langport West with a Taunton to Yeovil train.

c. 1911 Author's Collection

45XX class 2–6–2T No. 4593 arriving at Montacute with the 4.10 p.m. Yeovil (Pen Mill) to Taunton train. To the left of the engine is the post for holding the single line token that was collected by the fireman.

13.6.64 Hugh Ballantyne

BR Standard Class 3MT 2–6–2T No. 82044 arriving at Montacute with a Taunton to Yeovil train, allowing the permanent way man a rest from his task of re-sleepering. The platform has been rebuilt recently using standard concrete parts.

Lens of Sutton

The old passenger station at Hendford, later used for horse stabling, and then by the road motor engineer and his staff. The Southern Region has replaced the GWR lower quadrant signals with those of upper quadrant type.

Author's Collection

Creech Junction to Chard Junction

Plans for building the Chard branch date back to 1830, when some enterprising local people invited James Green, the County Surveyor for Devon, to make a report on the feasibility of building a canal linking Chard with the Bridgwater and Taunton Canal. Green carried out the survey, but suggested that a railway would be more in keeping with the times and a better business proposition. However his employers thought that they knew best and an Act for building a canal was obtained three years later, though the canal was not opened through to Chard until 1842.

During the Railway Mania in 1845 when so many wildcat schemes were put forward, Chard was mentioned in two plans for a rail link between the Bristol and English Channels. Such a scheme would naturally have taken traffic from the Bridgwater and Taunton, and Chard canals, so the waterway owners countered the suggestion with a railway of their own. Parliament refused to grant permission for a line, but sanctioned a railway from Creech to Ilminster. The Chard Canal Company immediately applied to Parliament to convert its waterway from Ilminster to Chard into a railway, the Act being duly passed the following year, 1847. The Chard Canal Company changed its name to the Chard Railway Company, but the only railway part of it was the title, for the concern was heavily in debt and had no funds to build a line.

The local people, quite undaunted, revived the proposal in 1852. An Act was passed the following year to convert the canal and extend the line to Taunton. Because of a lack of capital, this line also came to naught. In 1859 it was suggested at a meeting held in Chard that a short railway should be built linking the canal basin in the town with the LSWR's Exeter line, which was then under construction and passing only 3 miles to the south.

Parliament granted the necessary Act on 25 May 1860. Unfortunately the contractors engaged to construct the line, Messrs Payne & Furness, fell into difficulties and had to be released from their contract. Eventually another contractor, James Taylor, set to work, the first sod being cut on 1 November 1860 by Miss Susan Buckland. Soon, however, Taylor stopped work as he had fallen into the hands of creditors. Meanwhile Chard Road, later Chard Junction, on the main LSWR line, had been opened on 19 July 1860.

The LSWR supported the branch, and shares in the Chard Railway Company were sold by the local directors to LSWR nominees such as Charles Castleman, the Hon. Ralph Dutton, Edward J. Hutchins MP, H.C. Lacy and Wyndham Portal. Formal consent for the LSWR to take over the line was given by an Act of 22 June 1863.

On 8 May 1863 the inaugural train hauled by the 2–2–2WT No. 76 *Firefly* decorated with flowers, left Chard at 7.40 a.m. with twenty passengers, and after making a connection with a main line train, came back to Chard. The mayor and town council made a return journey on the next service, the 11.30 a.m. to Chard. When they arrived back they took luncheon in a marquee, the navvies feasting on beef and potatoes at the Red Lion.

The railway was not above criticism, some complaining that the third class fare of 4d. for a distance of 3 miles 110 yds was 'exhorbitant and abominable'. 2–2–2WT No. 13 *Orion*, built by Sharp Brothers in 1852, was the first regular branch engine, working it from 1863 until withdrawn in 1872.

Although this short line gave them some satisfaction, the people of Chard still looked towards a link with their county town. The outcome of this was the Chard and Taunton Railway Act of 1861 which gave both the B&ER and LSWR powers of subscription. The former were about the only investors, local people not wishing to chance their money, so a further Act came before Parliament the following year, permitting the B&ER to increase its subscription. Even this proved insufficient, so in 1863 the B&ER was granted an Act allowing it to take over the powers of the Chard and Taunton Company and to build a broad gauge line.

Lady Anna Gore Langton performed the ceremony of cutting the first sod early in September 1863. Logan & Rennie were the contractors and the engineer a local man, John Fox of Hatch. All the engineering works, including the 154 yd long Hatch tunnel, were built wide enough to accommodate double track, though only one was ever laid. This extension was opened to passengers on 11 September 1866, but as was the case on many local branch lines, the goods sheds were incomplete, so freight could not be carried until the following March.

A new joint station was constructed at Chard, the B&ER being responsible for its construction. It was designed with bay platforms at each end to keep the railways separate, no through running being possible because of the different gauges. In May 1867 the link at Chard between the B&ER and the LSWR was opened for the convenience of passengers, some of the LSWR's services from Chard Road being diverted into the Joint station, rather than the Chard Town terminus. However, so as not to inconvenience those passengers whose destination was nearer the Town station, a small platform and shelter were erected on the link line close to the Town station, from where tickets had to be obtained. Intermediate stations were at Hatch and Ilminster. Thorn, later Thornfalcon, was not opened until 1871.

When in 1878 the B&ER decided to convert its branches to standard gauge, it purposely kept the Chard branch broad gauge for as long as possible, in order to prevent the LSWR obtaining running powers over the line as far as Taunton. When the decision to finally abolish the broad gauge was taken, however, it was the first of the last group of lines to be converted. This was carried out on Sunday 19 July 1891, the 13 mile long branch being changed to standard gauge in only twenty hours. With this conversion, interchange of through traffic was now possible, though the demand was small. During the summer months, however, there was a weekly excursion from Taunton to Seaton. Formed of GWR stock, it was worked on from Chard Joint by an LSWR engine sent light from Yeovil Town.

On 30 December 1916 Chard Town station was closed as an economy measure, and from then onwards the LSWR left Chard to the GWR. The latter worked both branches from 1 January 1917, though from as early as 1896 the LSWR's Town station had been controlled by the GWR station-master, from his office at the Joint station.

A report issued by the GWR in 1925 gave interesting facts about the branch. The daily average of coal and mineral wagons sent and received was one and two respectively; figures for wagons of general goods were twelve and twenty-three; 626 wagons of livestock were carried over the branch that year and 83,789 milk churns were dealt with.

To combat bus competition, unstaffed halts were opened at Donyatt and Ilton on 5 and 26 May 1928 respectively. In the 1930s, when it became possible for more people to take a summer holiday, the branch had great possibilities of being developed as a through route between the Midlands and the resorts of Seaton, Sidmouth and Lyme Regis, but this chance was never seized.

During the Second World War the Taunton stop line was constructed from the Parrett estuary to Seaton. It consisted of 355 pill boxes, so that had the Germans invaded the south-western peninsula they could have been contained and prevented from spreading to the rest of the country. This defence line followed the Chard branch. The pill boxes were concealed: the one at Ilton was like a water tank, and that at Ilminster, a signal box. This camouflage was designed by Oliver Messel, a theatrical film designer.

Chard branch trains caused a problem to out-of-course main line traffic, as leaving the bay platform at Taunton they had to cross all the running lines and then had to cross back again at Creech junction.

Due to the national fuel crisis, the passenger service was suspended in February 1951 and many thought that it would never be reinstated, but, following strong protests from Chard, it was resumed in May. Passenger trains were insufficiently used, so the service was withdrawn from 10 September 1962, the goods service succumbing two years later on 6 July 1964. Thus Chard, formerly a town of two railways, became a town with no railways at all.

The descent from Chard to Chard junction was down a gradient of 1 in 80, and in the 1930s a 2–6–2T and two coaches failed to stop in time, demolished the buffers at Chard junction and ran into the road, a re-enactment of this taking place some twenty years later. On another occasion, when the congested yard at Chard Town was being shunted, in order to get the engine at the correct end the crew decided to fly shunt the brake van and three wagons. The locomotive hauled the brake van and three wagons for a short distance, then the engine was uncoupled and run into a siding, the shunter quickly pulling the points to allow the van and wagons to roll towards the branch. Although in theory this operation was a time-saver, in practice it was not without risk, and so it proved that day. In attempting to step on the running board of the brake van in order to enter and apply the brake, the shunter stumbled and nearly fell. He failed to mount the van and the train ran down the gradient to Chard junction, witnesses estimating that it reached about 40 mph before demolishing the buffer stops at the end of the GWR bay platform, passing through a fence, crossing the road and entering the car park of the Chard Road Hotel.

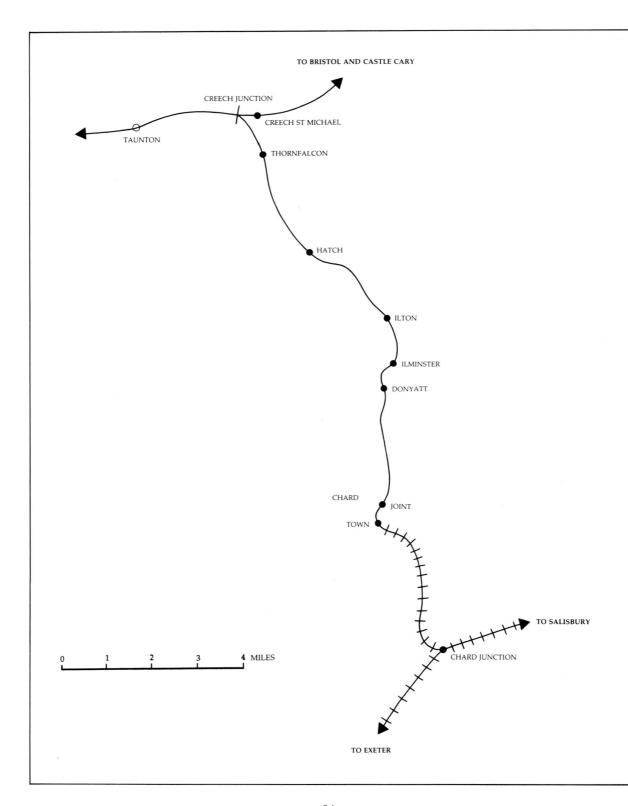

TO BRISTOL AND CASTLE CARY

CREECH JUNCTION

CREECH ST MICHAEL

TAUNTON

THORNFALCON

HATCH

ILTON

ILMINSTER

DONYATT

CHARD

JOINT

TOWN

TO SALISBURY

CHARD JUNCTION

0 1 2 3 4 MILES

TO EXETER

B&ER broad gauge 4–4–0ST No. 25 on the turntable at Yeovil.

c. 1860 Dr A.J.G. Dickens / Author's Collection

Thornfalcon, view 'Up'. Notice the track on bridge rail, the timber platforms and buildings. The station was curious in that passengers had to cross a goods siding to gain access.

c. 1905 Lens of Sutton

Building an overbridge at Thornfalcon. The contractor's line is still in place.

c. 1865 Author's Collection

Hatch station, view 'Up' towards the 152 yd long tunnel. The siding on the right is on longitudinal sleepers.

c. 1905 Author's Collection

8750 class 0–6–0PT No. 3787 leaves Hatch station and passes the goods shed.

18.8.62 S.P.J.A. Derek

8750 class 0–6–0PT No. 4612, now preserved by Swindon Railway Engineering, with the 2.42 p.m. Saturdays-only Taunton to Chard Central arrives at Ilminster.

27.5.61 R.E. Toop

8750 class 0–6–0PT No. 8783 arrives at Donyatt Halt with a train for Taunton. Unstaffed, the halt was supervised by the Ilminster station-master.

8.9.62 Author's Collection

At Chard Central an unidentified 0–6–0PT heads a train towards Taunton, while an oncoming train headed by a 45XX 2–6–2T waits by the signal box until the platform is free. Part of the train shed can be seen. Notice the 'mushroom' type water tank at the end of the platform and the grain hopper wagon in the siding.

28.4.62 E. Wilmshurst

Chard Town goods, formerly the LSWR's passenger station. The platform has been lengthened at some time, for the slope of the platform ramp can be seen on the wall. Notice the use of old sleepers to separate the various grades of fuel.

28.4.62 E. Wilmshurst

Tartar class 2–2–2WT No. 13 *Orion* heads an LSWR train in the bay platform at Chard Joint. A little of the train shed can be seen on the extreme right. The mixed gauge was only within the station area.

c. 1867 Author's Collection

Norton Fitzwarren to Minehead

The first scheme to connect Minehead with a railway was put forward in 1833, when a horse-worked line was proposed from Minehead to Tiverton and Exeter. Nothing came of this idea and the next scheme was the Somersetshire and North Devon Junction Railway, in 1845. With John Hughes as engineer, it was planned to build a line from the B&ER at Bridgwater to Minehead and Ilfracombe, giving a sea connection with Ireland. That same year an associated line, the Bristol & English Channels Direct Junction Railway, was proposed from Bridport to Watchet. The plans fell through, however, not even getting as far as an Act of Parliament.

In the 1850s a line between Bridgwater and Watchet was favoured, but the Quantocks formed a barrier to a direct route and the cost of tunnelling would have been prohibitive, though a Bridgwater to Watchet line was still being suggested as recently as 1923. The alternative of a railway from the main line at Norton Fitzwarren seemed more feasible.

Influential landowners met at Williton on 9 July 1856 to promote a line between the B&ER near Taunton, Williton, and the West Somerset Mineral Railway then in course of construction from the iron ore mines on the Brendon Hills. A committee was formed to get the best plan for a railway from the engineers. A few weeks later, on 27 October 1856, a meeting was held in the Guildhall, Taunton, for the purpose of promoting the West Somerset Railway, pledging to support the directors and engineer, giving them *carte blanche* to do what they thought fit. This engineer was I.K. Brunel, and it proved to be one of his final undertakings.

In view of the forthcoming railway, Watchet expected an increased trade from Bridgwater: bricks, general pottery, cement and other products from the alluvial deposits of the River Parrett, as Watchet offered the shortest sea route to the western part of South Wales and avoided the treacherous and tortuous navigation of the river below Bridgwater. To cope with this anticipated increase of shipping, an extension of Watchet harbour was sought to include a new breakwater giving an area of about 10 acres of harbour where vessels could float at all states of the tide.

The West Somerset Railway had intended to make a junction with the West Somerset Mineral Railway, but a difficulty arose over the right of building a railway on the pier. The directors decided against the junction when Brunel advised that it would bring the railway to a level unsuited to any westward extension.

The first meeting of the WSR was held in Taunton on 10 February 1858. The B&ER undertook to work the completed line, provide plant and maintain the branch at a rental of 45 per cent of gross receipts, with a minimum guarantee of £4,000 per annum. It was estimated that the guarantee would pay 3 per cent on the outlay.

At the next meeting the secretary reported that the permanent way survey was almost complete, and that some of the landowners' agents had made unreasonable claims for compensation. As this increased the cost of the line, a new agreement was made with the

B&ER which agreed to lease the line in perpetuity and pay the WSR 55 per cent of the gross receipts with a guarantee of £4,500 per annum.

The ceremony of turning the first sod took place at Crowcombe on 7 April 1859 and the contractor, George Furness of London, started work three days later. As some of the shares were taken up rather reluctantly, work proceeded slowly, and it took nearly three years before the 14$\frac{1}{2}$ miles of broad gauge line were opened. On 15 September 1859 Brunel died, and was succeeded by his chief assistant, R.P. Brereton.

The railway was sufficiently advanced for a locomotive to travel over the line on 6 March 1862, and the Board of Trade inspector paid a visit two days later. His report was satisfactory; indeed some of the original rails lasted at Crowcombe until 1923. The ceremonial opening was held on 29 March and the line opened to the general public on 31 March. Four trains ran each way on weekdays, and two on Sundays. At first the line was only used by passenger trains because the goods sheds were not ready until August.

On 1 September 1863 a special fifteen coach excursion was run from Taunton to Watchet, carrying 1,000 passengers for a boat trip to Ilfracombe. Unfortunately one of the three steamers to carry them onwards failed to materialize, and 300 of the trippers had to remain at Watchet.

An extension of the WSR from Watchet to Minehead was authorized on 5 July 1865. It was to be built by a local company, the Minehead Railway, under the auspices of the Somerset and Dorset Railway. As insufficient capital was raised, the company was dissolved in 1870. It was reconstituted on 29 June 1871 by an Act of Parliament and had R.P. Brereton as engineer. Its ruling gradient was 1 in 65 – quite steep for a railway – and this extended for over a mile between Blue Anchor and Washford.

During the building of this extension, serious labour problems arose, and at one point navvies were only kept out of the clerk of works' office at the point of a loaded revolver. The 8$\frac{1}{4}$ miles of broad gauge line were opened on 16 July 1874. Horse drawn coaches ran a connecting service between Minehead and Lynton at least until 1910.

In August 1878 it was recommended that the branch should be converted to standard gauge as soon as possible, to save the cost of transferring goods on to broad gauge wagons at Taunton and also relieve the shortage of broad gauge wagons which was becoming acute, as the company did not wish to build new stock in view of the gauge's eventual abolition. The 22$\frac{3}{4}$ miles of track were attacked by 500 men in seven gangs of seventy at daybreak on Sunday 29 October 1882, with such vigour that soon after midday a standard gauge special with the divisional engineer and traffic superintendent was able to get through to Minehead. The next day one passenger train ran in each direction, and on Tuesday morning the normal service was resumed.

The Minehead Railway was taken over by the GWR in 1897 after that company had acquired all its capital. The GWR had to reach its possession over WSR metals, for the latter retained independence until 1922.

The 1926 statistics give the average number of coal and mineral wagons received on the branch daily as eighteen inwards and one outwards; thirty-seven wagons of general goods received and thirty-one dispatched; while annually there were 1,064 livestock trucks and 7,165 milk churns.

Minehead's population rose from less than 2,000 when the railway arrived, to 6,000 in 1931 and over 8,000 today. With the advent of workers' holidays the district became a tourist area, and to accelerate train working on the single line, two extra crossing loops were opened in 1933 and automatic token exchangers provided to enable locomotives to collect a token at speeds of up to 40 mph. When exchange was by hand they were restricted to 15 mph.

These token exchangers were based on a type invented by Alfred Whitaker, Locomotive Superintendent of the S&DR. An iron post had two arms parallel with the line and on a train's approach, was swung at right angles. These jaws with two teeth above and below faced the train, and the impact forced the handle of the tough leather token pouch on the engine's apparatus into the jaws. On the lower arm was a half cup on which the token for the section ahead was resting, and this was collected by a similar apparatus on the engine. To speed working still further, the line was doubled between Dunster and Minehead in 1933, and the platforms of many of the stations lengthened. Norton Fitzwarren to Bishops Lydeard was doubled three years later.

In 1934, each Sunday from 6 May until 24 June, a Holiday Haunts Express was run from Bath, Bristol and Weston-Super-Mare to Watchet, Dunster and Minehead. Sufficient time was given to passengers to book their apartments for a longer visit later in the season. Fares for this special train varied from 5s. to 10s.

The GWR started camp coaches in 1934, one of the first being at Blue Anchor. Passengers purchasing railway tickets to the station could hire the coach for accommodation for a very reasonable sum.

The opening of Butlin's holiday camp at Minehead in 1962 increased the summer passenger traffic, and as many as 2,000 long distance passengers were handled on a peak summer Saturday. Freight on the branch ceased in 1964 and was distributed by road from Taunton. Esparto grass was brought to Watchet harbour for paper making. When the *Flamenco* sailed in from Panama, its cargo of 1,450 tons required 351 railway wagons.

To avoid delaying main line trains by shunting movements at Taunton, at one period branch trains were run through from Minehead to Yeovil. 'Bulldog' class tender engines gave drivers a more comfortable ride than the tank engines, but at the end of the journey, the footplate crew were faced with the hard task of manually pushing the engine round on the turntables at Yeovil and Minehead. Both turntables were badly balanced as, being short, they had been lengthened with hinged extensions on which a tender was run up at a steep angle.

One Sunday evening during the Second World War, Driver G. Smith and Fireman Jack Gardner took 2–6–2T No. 4136 and nine empty coaches to Watchet to carry USA troops to Taunton on the first leg of their journey, probably to the south coast. On arrival at Watchet, No. 4136 was run round the train and then reversed to the goods sheds to pick up two loaded Syphon G bogie vans and two bogie flat wagons with two anti-aircraft guns on each. The load behind No. 4136 was now thirteen vehicles and weighed a total of approximately 400 tons. An American officer asked if he could ride on the footplate with the crew as he doubted the capabilities of No. 4136 to handle such a load. He was amazed when she romped up the six mile long bank of 1 in 92 from Williton to Crowcombe . . . and so was the fireman!

Leigh Wood Crossing, Crowcombe, was where in 1913 one of the very few women was concerned in traffic operations on a British railway. When employed by the GWR at Chard, in 1880 Mrs Hill's husband met with a serious accident. He was transferred to the relatively light job at Leigh Wood Crossing, but was never again fit for duty. His wife undertook his work operating the crossing gates and carried it out so efficiently that, after his death in 1881, she was allowed to remain in charge.

Simultaneous departures from Norton Fitzwarren at 8.28 a.m. of trains from Barnstaple and Minehead, the former on the relief and the latter on the main line, proved exciting. Both trains were due at Taunton at 8.35. Schoolboys and girls sometimes adopted the highly dangerous practice of leaning out and holding hands between trains.

From 26 February 1968 economies were made on the Minehead branch when, except at terminal stations, passengers obtained their tickets from the guard. Even so, the line was not found to be economic and the last train ran on 2 January 1971. Fortunately this was far from being the end of the story, as the first section of the preserved WSR was reopened from Minehead to Blue Anchor on 28 March 1976 and through to Bishops Lydeard on 9 June 1979, with a very occasional train running through from BR, a limit being put on the number of trains using Taunton Cider Company's interchange which is essential for such working. In 1991 the WSR carried 116,573 passengers.

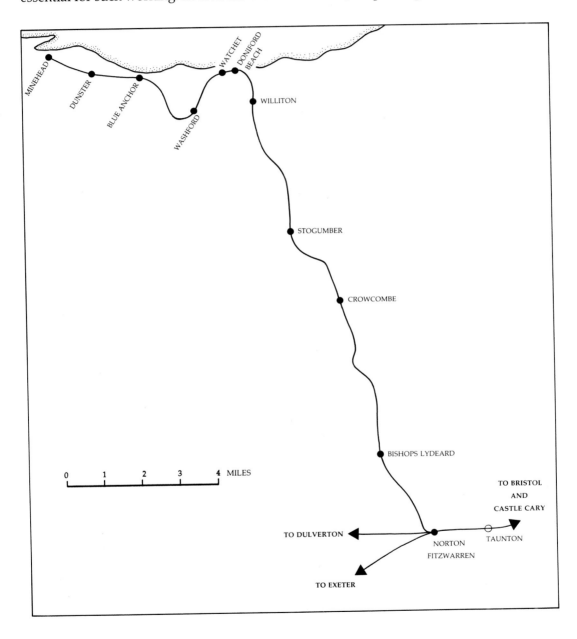

2201 class 0–6–0 No. 2215 of Taunton shed with an ex-ROD tender, at Norton Fitzwarren with a Taunton to Minehead train. Notice the mass of point rodding.

6.9.47 Roger Venning

5101 class 2–6–2T No. 5172 taking the Minehead branch at Norton Fitzwarren, heading a Paddington to Minehead through train. The white target with 'M' on it helped signalmen differentiate between Minehead and Barnstaple trains.

6.9.47 Roger Venning

Evacuees from London arrive at Williton during the first weekend of the Second World War. Some people are carrying gas masks.

Author's Collection

A broad gauge B&ER 4–4–0ST braving the floods at Williton. Note the permanent way hand trolley in the right foreground.

1877 Author's Collection

A wall-mounted gas lamp to illuminate the platform at Williton. Notice the two wires hanging down from the crank: pulling one turned it on and the other turned it off.

28.8.67 D. Payne

A Southern Railway wagon being loaded with coal at Watchet Harbour from a coaster. Apart from the LNWR wagon in the foreground, all the others are post-grouping. The card was postmarked 1 September 1936.

Author's Collection

B&ER 4–4–0ST No. 74 on the turntable at Watchet in the days when Watchet was a terminus, because the line to Minehead had yet to be opened. This engine was built by the Vulcan Foundry in 1867, became GWR No. 2047 in 1876 and was scrapped with the end of the broad gauge in 1892. It was sister engine to No. 2051 which, while heading an 'Up' special express, ran at full speed into a goods train at Norton Fitzwarren on 11 November 1890.

c. 1870 H.H. Hole

B&ER 4–4–0ST No. 68 at Watchet. Built by the Vulcan Foundry in 1867, it was withdrawn in 1880. This picture was taken before vacuum brakes were fitted to passenger trains, the only brake power being provided by handbrakes on the engine and guard's van. Notice that only the lower half of the smoke box door is hinged. A re-railing jack is carried each side of the engine.

c. 1870 H.H. Hole

Ex-S&DJR 2–8–0 No. 88 being restored at Washford on the preserved West Somerset Railway. It returned to service in September 1987 in BR livery, numbered 53808.

1.6.78 Author

43XX class 2–6–0 No. 6398 of Taunton shed, leaves Blue Anchor with a Taunton to Minehead train. The gradient post on the right indicates a steepening in the gradient from 1 in 229 to 1 in 91 in the 'Down' direction.

17.2.49 Pursey Short

A DMU driver's view leaving Blue Anchor for Dunster. Camping coaches are parked on the siding to the left, just beyond the level crossing.

1.2.69 W.H. Harbor / Author's Collection

The preserved West Somerset Railway on a misty morning. 64XX class 0–6–0PT No. 6412 reaches the head of the 1 in 91 gradient up to Blue Anchor, hauling the 10.35 a.m. from Minehead.

1.6.78 Author

An early engraving in broad gauge days showing the proximity of Minehead station to the beach.

c. 1875 Author's Collection

A varied assortment of horse drawn vehicles outside Minehead station waiting to take passengers on to their destination – perhaps to Lynton or another village, or to hotels and boarding houses in the town.

c. 1905 Author's Collection

The goods and passenger station at Minehead. The assortment of rolling stock includes vehicles belonging to the LNWR, Cheshire Lines Committee, the Midland Railway and Cannock and Rugeley Colliery.

15.6.23 GWR

Minehead in preservation days. Left to right: ex-GWR No. 6412, Peckett built 1163 *Whitehead* and ex-LBSCR 'Terrier' No. 32678. The latter is now preserved on the Kent & East Sussex Railway.

1.6.78 Author

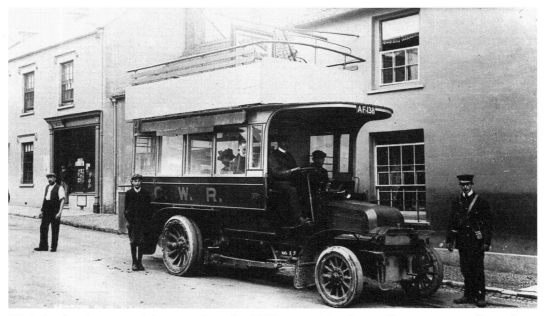

With the development of the motor bus, the GWR ran services from villages not served by rail – a far cheaper expedient than laying a light railway. Here is 20 hp Milnes–Daimler GWR Fleet No. 20 at Nether Stowey. The vehicle first came into service on 6 July 1905. The driver is E. Hancock.

1908 Author's Collection

Norton Fitzwarren to Dulverton

The Devon and Somerset Railway, a line promoted by landowners between Norton Fitzwarren and Barnstaple, received its Act of Parliament on 29 July 1864. In the same year the contractor started work at Barnstaple, but was almost immediately replaced by another. By August 1866 the route from Norton Fitzwarren to Wiveliscombe was staked out, but that month the contractors were forced to discharge their men, as the DSR was unable to make cash payments for the work done. The stoppage was only for a few days and work was quickly resumed. Towards the end of the month, two navvies fell ill with cholera and in an effort to prevent it from spreading, pitch fires were lit in every street. Whether or not this was efficacious, certainly only a few caught it.

As the DSR again failed to pay its account on 29 September 1866, Messrs Pickering suspended work for an indefinite period and paid off all local employees. The railway works lay untouched for almost four years until 11 May 1870, when the contract was given to John Langham Reed. This meeting was also memorable for the fact that it was attended by Eugenius Birch. He had been dismissed from his post as the company's engineer some seventeen months previously as he had proved incapable of superintending the line. When asked to leave the meeting he refused, only going when the directors threatened to send for the police.

On 8 June 1871 the branch opened from Norton junction, as Norton Fitzwarren was then called, to Wiveliscombe, with an intermediate station at Milverton, the latter town having most of the decorations and celebrations. Two bands played, unfortunately in close proximity.

The adage of 'cheap proving dear' was certainly the case with the contractor. Time showed that the permanent way was of poor quality and many rails had to be replaced. The fencing, too, required much work to keep it in good order.

In 1872 Richard Hassard, the DSR engineer, had a conversation with Henry Ellis, a B&ER director, relating to the gauge of the line and if the DSR directors had realized the full import of this conversation, they could have saved the thousands of pounds which the gauge conversion cost. Ellis said that a great change had taken place in the feeling of his board regarding the broad gauge, and that if the DSR approached the B&ER directors it might be possible to change the gauge. Unfortunately the DSR directors ignored this hint and continued laying the more expensive broad gauge, only to be told two and a half years later that the B&ER had resolved to convert its lines to standard gauge. This, of course, meant that the DSR had to follow suit.

Meanwhile work on the line between Wiveliscombe and Barnstaple had been proceeding. This section had several major engineering works, those in Somerset being Bathealton Tunnel, 445 yds, Venn Cross Viaduct, 159 yds and Venn Cross Tunnel, 246 yds. The line opened on 1 November 1873 and from 1 August 1876 the B&ER was amalgamated with the GWR, so the latter took over working the DSR. On 16 September 1880 the agreement with the GWR for narrowing the gauge was sealed. Platelayers were brought in from other districts to assist with the conversion, which took place between 15–17 May 1881, the last broad gauge train running over the line on Saturday 14 May. A standard gauge goods and two passenger trains ran on 18 May, the full service operating from the following day.

Ordinary shareholders saw that their line would never make a profit and so sold it to the GWR on 1 July 1901.

In 1917–18 the branch was the scene of trials of experimental concrete sleepers. Trains run over them were subject to a speed limit of 30 mph but few sleepers lasted more than nine years.

In the summers before the First World War, the Ilfracombe portion of the Torbay Express, which had been slipped from the rest of the train at Taunton, ran over the branch. It was the only slip portion in history to include a restaurant car in its four coach formation. Another interesting train was the daily rabbit special from South Molton, but myxomatosis put a halt to this traffic.

As on the Minehead branch, automatic token exchangers were fitted to locomotives in the 1930s. They were not an unqualified success as the apparatus was not entirely reliable, engines shaking sideways under load, or a depression of a rail, causing the catcher to miss. On one occasion a token flew off the catcher into a field of wheat, and was lost for a time.

Bathealton Tunnel caused problems to locomotive crews. One 'Bulldog' class 4–4–0 with a passenger train slipped to a standstill, and the driver and fireman were overcome by fumes. On regaining consciousness, they found they were out of the tunnel and rolling backwards towards Wiveliscombe. They halted the train, made another attempt and succeeded. Drivers tried various techniques approaching the tunnel. Some sanded the rail before entering, but as there was a curve before the tunnel mouth, this retarded the train's progress. Other drivers took their chance and did not apply sand unless the engine slipped. At least one driver sanded just the straight rail before the tunnel and never experienced problems.

Venn Cross viaduct was not strong enough to support the weight of two engines unless separated by a tender. This meant that if a tank engine was piloting a tender engine, the tank engine had to be uncoupled and run over the viaduct first, unless the second engine was working tender-first.

In 1944, just before D-Day, certain railway locations were guarded as it was thought that the enemy might destroy them in order to delay the invasion. Venn Cross viaduct was protected by the Home Guard. On one single day in May 1944, no less than fifteen troop trains arrived in Dulverton, each carrying 1,000 men and vast stores of food.

To facilitate crossings on the branch, the section from Norton Fitzwarren to Milverton was doubled in 1937; at the same time the junction at Norton Fitzwarren was repositioned so that it connected with the main line instead of the Minehead branch. Although busy in the Second World War, with the increase in road transport afterwards, the branch became uneconomic and closed on 1 October 1966.

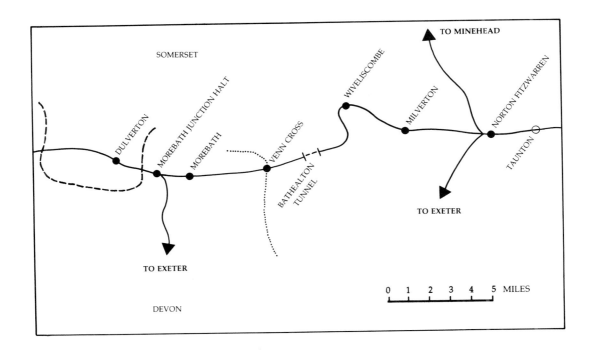

TO MINEHEAD

SOMERSET

WIVELISCOMBE

MILVERTON

NORTON FITZWARREN

DULVERTON

MOREBATH JUNCTION HALT

MOREBATH

VENN CROSS

BATHEALTON TUNNEL

TAUNTON

TO EXETER

TO EXETER

DEVON

0   1   2   3   4   5   MILES

Milverton station in broad gauge days before doubling. Notice the 'Down' disc and crossbar signal at danger. Beside it is the flag signal indicating 'Caution'.

c. 1881 Author's Collection

SR N class 2–6–0 No. 31406 heading the 8.02 a.m. Wolverhampton to Ilfracombe train nearing Wiveliscombe.

25.7.64 P.W. Gray

43XX class 2–6–0 No. 7333 near Wiveliscombe with the 1.05 p.m. Taunton to Barnstaple.

1.5.62 David Holmes

The signalman and driver exchange single line tokens at Wiveliscombe. The engine is diesel-hydraulic D6332.

August 1965 D. Payne

Wiveliscombe to Milverton single line token.

The 264 yd long Venn Cross tunnel from the station.

c. 1966 D. Payne

'Up' train at Venn Cross. The gradient of 1 in 58 down at the far end of the station is quite noticeable. The county boundary between Somerset and Devon ran between the signal box and the goods shed situated behind the cameraman. The station offices were at the top of the cutting instead of on the platform.

c. 1935 Lens of Sutton

Results of a runaway on a gradient of 1 in 60 near Venn Cross.

May 1948 Author's Collection

43XX class 2–6–0 No. 6398 at Venn Cross with a 'Down' goods.

21.6.58 R.J. Sellick

The 159 yd long Venn Cross viaduct.

c. 1874 Author's Collection

43XX class No. 6346 arrives at Dulverton with a 'Down' stopping train, crossing a sister engine heading an 'Up' train. Centre is an 0–4–2T with the Exe Valley auto.

T.J. Saunders

SR N class No. 31842 at Dulverton with an 'Up' train. The Exe Valley auto is on the left.
c. 1958 M.E.J. Deane

2251 class 0–6–0 No. 2266 at Wiveliscombe with an 'Up' train composed of an SR set. The engine carries a 'B' plate. Notice the bars protecting the signal box locking room windows.
c. 1958 M.E.J. Deane

Castle Cary to Yeovil

Although at one time the line from Castle Cary to Yeovil and Weymouth was certainly a main line, today it is no more than a branch.

The broad gauge, single track, Wilts, Somerset and Weymouth Railway from Frome to Yeovil opened on 1 September 1856 and was narrowed on 18–22 June 1874. To cope with increasing traffic, it was doubled in 1881. As early as 1935 the line was scheduled for GWR diesel railcars allocated to Bristol, St Philip's March shed, running a Bristol to Weymouth service, a top speed of 80 mph being possible, but full dieselization of the line did not come until 6 April 1959. With the development of road services and the need for economy, the line between Castle Cary and Yeovil was reduced to a single track on 12 May 1968, the intermediate stations of Sparkford and Marston Magna having closed on 3 October 1966. What once had been a busy main line was now a mere branch with a reduced train service.

In July 1938, when Castle Cary to Yeovil was very much a main line, twelve passenger trains were scheduled on weekdays, some through to and from London, Wolverhampton and Bristol, while on summer Saturdays there was one to and from Cardiff. Every summer until 26 September 1959, the Channel Islands boat express ran on weekdays from Paddington to Weymouth Quay. Regular Paddington to Weymouth through services ended in 1960, two years after the Southern Region took over operating control of the Castle Cary to Weymouth line.

Much of the Channel Island market garden produce was landed at Weymouth and was carried over the Yeovil to Castle Cary line. In 1912, 124 special potato trains were run between 1 May and 24 June earning an income of £19,062. At the height of the season tomato traffic demanded up to five specials a day, in addition to traffic carried by ordinary services. These specials had the code name Perpots (perishables and potatoes). In addition to the passengers and freight to and from Weymouth and the Channel Islands, the line carried traffic to and from the Royal Naval base at Portland. In coal-burning days the Navy required many truckloads of fuel.

The current passenger timetable shows nine trains each way daily, all commencing at Cardiff or Bristol, except one from Worcester on Spring Bank Holiday Monday, and on Mondays to Fridays throughout the school summer holidays.

When the Westbury MAS signalling extension was being carried out in 1985, the track layout at Castle Cary was altered to provide an independent Weymouth platform line signalled in both directions; thus the 'Down' platform became an island. This innovation was all the more remarkable as the Taunton steam railmotors had always been dealt with at the main line platforms, and in the present day pattern Weymouth line trains do not originate or terminate at Castle Cary.

Sparkford possessed a dairy with siding connection, which from 1932 until 1963 generated useful revenue from milk traffic, in milk tanks.

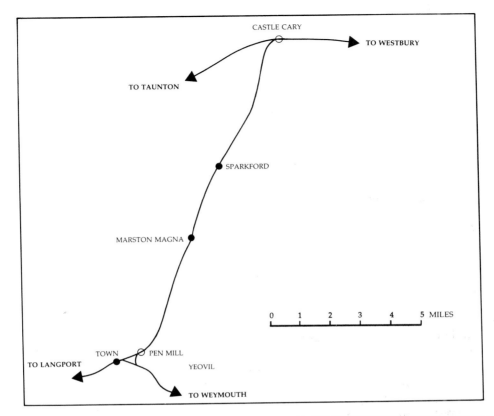

Yeovil Pen Mill looking 'Up', showing the rather curious layout with a platform on each side of a single track. The train is the 1414 Bristol (Temple Meads) to Weymouth consisting of two three-car units, the power cars of the first being W51446 and W51517.

4.8.81 Author

Yeovil Junction to Yeovil Town

Yeovil owed much of its success to the fact that it was a well-served railway centre. In 1909 it had fourteen glove factories, a large butter, cheese and potted meat factory, a foundry, large engineering works, motor works and important printing and newspaper establishments, all in addition to being an agricultural centre and market town.

Because the LSWR skirted the town to the south, about eighteen trains ran each way daily over the one and three quarter miles between Yeovil Junction and Yeovil Town, connecting with all main line expresses. To avoid the branch engine having to uncouple and run round at the end of each short journey, they were generally push-pull worked, the engine pulling normally in one direction and then pushing on its return journey, the driver controlling the engine from a special compartment at what was now the front of the train. Until 1963 these were of the SR type, but that year ex-GWR engines and auto cars were introduced.

Yeovil Town station was owned jointly by the LSWR and the B&ER, later taken over by the GWR. Opened 1 June 1861, it was built in red brick with creamy ashlar dressings, the Tudor façade having projecting wings and a large central gable. The three platforms were covered by train sheds, later removed. When opened, the stations had four signal boxes: one each for the B&ER and LSWR duplicated at either end of the station. A station-master's house was at each end of the station, for each company had its own man in charge. The original four signal boxes were replaced by just two boxes on 26 October 1902, and these in turn were replaced by one on 15 October 1916.

The station was manned by three different staffs: the LSWR, GWR and Joint. Each company's staff attended to the traffic of its own railway and assisted with transfers from one railway to another, while the Joint staff, consisting of five signal men, a lamp boy and a waiting room attendant, were responsible for the work of both railways. The GWR was responsible for the permanent way and signalling, while the LSWR attended to the building's fabric.

Adjacent to the station was an LSWR three-road red brick locomotive shed. In 1909 twenty-three engines were allocated, its staff consisting of one foreman, two clerks, thirty drivers, twenty-seven firemen, one cleaners' chargeman, twenty-one cleaners, three fitters' lads and one boilersmith. The introduction of diesels rendered the depot redundant and it closed in June 1965.

Following closure of the Cirencester and Tetbury branches, two of the four railbuses used on these services were utilized on the Yeovil Junction to Yeovil Town shuttle from 28 December 1964. Shorter than a conventional diesel railcar, they ran on four, rather than eight, wheels, though seating forty-six passengers and allowing space for luggage. Even with these economical vehicles the service was not considered to be paying its way, and it was withdrawn on 2 October 1966.

M7 class 0–4–4T No. 129 enters Yeovil Town station with the push-pull train from Yeovil Junction.
21.9.46 Pursey Short

M7 class 0–4–4T No. 30131, of 72C Yeovil shed, at Yeovil Town with the 10.50 a.m. Saturdays-only Yeovil Town to Yeovil Junction.

2.7.60 David Holmes

General view of Yeovil Town station, with the locomotive shed on the far right.

c. 1956 M.E.J. Deane

64XX class 0–6–0PT No. 6419 en route between Yeovil Town and Yeovil Junction. Yeovil South Junction signal box can be seen in the distance where the line from Pen Mill to Weymouth starts to run parallel with that from Yeovil Town.

11.7.64 E. Wilmshurst

An AC Cars four-wheel railbus at Yeovil Junction working the shuttle service to Yeovil Town.

1965 D. Payne

Kelston to Bath

Kelston to Bath was the Somerset section of the Mangotsfield to Bath branch, the Gloucestershire section being described in *Branch Lines of Gloucestershire* by Colin G. Maggs, published by Alan Sutton in 1991.

The double tracked branch opened on 4 August 1869, and grew in importance when the Somerset and Dorset Railway was extended to Bath in 1874. The branch enjoyed steady freight traffic throughout the year and particularly heavy passenger traffic on summer Saturdays when holiday-makers were going to and from the south coast.

A feature of the branch was the six attractive latticework bridges over the Avon. In 1933 a scheme was initiated for strengthening the line so that heavier engines could use it. Five of the large bridges were replaced by those of the box girder pattern, but the replacement of the bridge outside Bath station would have caused too much disturbance to railway traffic, so it was strengthened at every joint by welding.

The large goods station at Bath was built on Sydenham Field and, curiously enough, on 30 June 1864 as the House of Commons Committee was discussing the Bath extension, W.G. Grace, then fifteen years of age, first played for the All-England Eleven against the Eighteen of Lansdown, this match taking place on Sydenham Field.

Another interesting feature of the branch was that near the locomotive depot, a siding led to a wharf beside the Avon. This was used for rail/barge exchange and at least five MR barges were registered at Bath. They travelled along the Kennet and Avon Canal, owned by the GWR since 1852.

Until about 1930 race trains from the north stopped at Kelston, and about half their passengers opted to get out and walk up to the racecourse on Lansdown instead of going on into the city and obtaining transport. The walk from Kelston station to the racecourse was only 2 $1/2$ miles, but included a climb of 700 ft.

On racedays there were plenty of railway police in evidence as bookies and punters tried to avoid paying their fares, while it was not unknown for welshing bookmakers to run across the fields and hide in bushes by Kelston station, only leaping into an 'Up' train as it was about to start.

The local squire was allowed to have expresses stopped for him at Kelston, this being a condition under which the station was built. Its position was unusual inasmuch as there was no roadway, access being across three quarters of a mile of fields. Latterly mainly used by anglers, it closed on 31 December 1948. Its signal box was only opened on summer Saturdays to shorten the block section from Bitton to Weston.

Weston station had its local traffic siphoned off when Bath Electric Tramways opened in 1904, and only a dozen passengers used it daily when it closed on 21 September 1953. Passenger traffic was withdrawn from the entire branch on 7 March 1966. This rendered the double track superfluous, one line being closed 5 May 1968. With the introduction of supplies from the North Sea, Bath gas works closed in May 1971; and the branch which had only remained open to provide the works with about forty wagons of coal each day, closed on 28 May 1971.

At first horses had drawn wagons over the siding to the gas works, but from 1901 a steam engine was used, the first being an Aveling and Porter geared locomotive, and the second and third, Peckett and Avonside 0–4–0 saddle tanks. In 1964 the second-hand Ruston and Hornsby four-wheel diesel-mechanical engines were purchased. When snow thawed and re-froze forming an ice block in a wagon, making it almost impossible to extract the coal, Bath gas works had the unusual method of thawing it by placing a tray of burning coke beneath.

Permanent way gangs, in addition to keeping the track in order, were also responsible for maintaining the land up to the company's boundary. Before setting fire to a bank to burn the dried grass, the area near the boundary first required controlled burning to act as a fire break. One man in the Weston gang took less care than he should, resulting in a cherry tree catching alight in an adjacent garden. The owner succeeded in claiming £14 damages from the railway. A few years later the same gardener asked the permanent way men if they would burn it down again because it had made his tree give a heavier crop!

The Midland station at Bath, its Georgian façade admirably matching the city's main style of architecture, was preserved, together with the 66 ft span train shed. It has subsequently been developed as a supermarket. Not many Bathonians were aware that until 1967, the station had spacious cellars, in which spirits were kept until the bonded warehouse closed.

The withdrawal of train services by BR has not meant that the branch is no longer of use. The Bristol Suburban Railway Society, now the Avon Valley Railway, reopened Bitton station in 1972 and have relaid track to Oldland Common and hope in due course to reach the outskirts of Bath at Newbridge. Its stud of about ten steam locomotives varies from main line engines to industrial shunters.

Another development in the use of the branch has been that from Rudmore Park, in the western suburbs of Bath, to Mangotsfield, became a walkway and cycle track in 1979. An unusual feature is that, to create additional interest, a series of sculptures is being created along the path. Most are dual purpose, serving as seats or drinking fountains as well as being works of art.

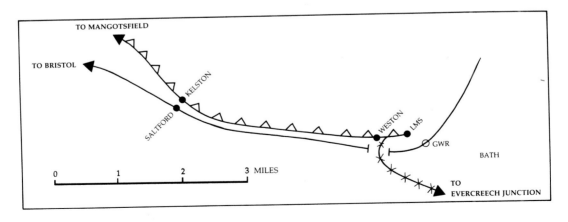

Advert from the *Bath & Wilts Evening Chronicle* of 23 March 1934.

Class 8F 2–8–0 No. 48737, of 82F Bath (Green Park) shed, with an 'Up' freight near Kelston Park.
16.6.64 Author

A rare view of a weed-killing train composed of ex-LNWR tenders, on the 'Up' line west of Bath. It is headed by a Class 4F 0–6–0.

2.6.49 Author

Class 2MT 2–6–2T No. 41241, of 71G Bath (Green Park) shed, leaving Weston with the 6.10 p.m. Bath to Bristol (St Phillip's). This was the last 'Up' train to stop at this station.

19.9.53 Author

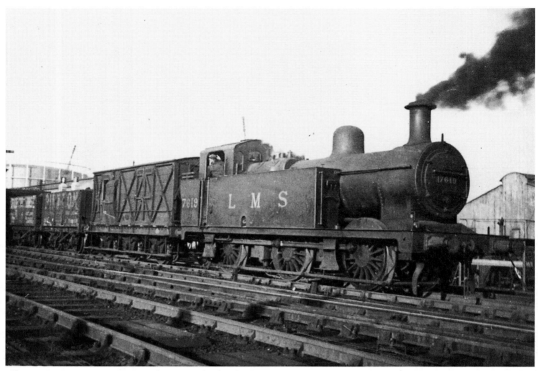

Class 3F 0–6–0T No. 7619, of 22C Bath shed, shunting at Bath with a Somerset and Dorset mail van behind the bunker.

c. 1935 S. Miles Davey, courtesy Peter Davey

Class 3P 2–6–2T No. 40164 passing Bath (Green Park) MPD with the 3.35 p.m. to Bristol (St Phillip's).

23.10.51 Hugh Ballantyne

Ex-GWR 4–6–0 No. 7813 *Freshford Manor* outside the Midland Railway engine shed at Bath. It had arrived on a pigeon special. On the left is Class 4F 0–6–0 No. 44169.

13.5.61 Rev. Alan Newman

In an unsuccessful trial, former London, Tilbury and Southend Railway 4–4–2T No. 62 *Camden Road*, is seen at Bath as LMS No. 2103 with a train to Mangotsfield. A former Pullman car is in the left background.

16.7.36 Rev. Alan Newman

Latterly diesel-electric locomotives worked Bath to Bristol local trains. Here is Peak class D116 with the 5.55 p.m. Bath (Green Park) to Bristol (Temple Meads), leaving Bath (Green Park station). To the left is the HM Customs and Excise Bonded Stores.

28.4.62 R.E. Toop

HM Customs and Excise Bonded Stores on the platform of Bath (Green Park) station. Spirits were stored in cellars beneath the station.

20.12.67 Author

A very early picture of the classical façade of the Midland Railway's terminus at Bath, now occupied by J. Sainsbury's supermarket.

c. 1870 Author's Collection

Evercreech Junction to Burnham-on-Sea

As long ago as 1851, the inhabitants of Glastonbury wanted a railway to carry their goods to the sea at Highbridge. The scheme depended on the good will of the B&ER, the owner of the existing Glastonbury Navigation and Canal which ran between Glastonbury and Highbridge harbour. The B&ER was generous and offered the canal in return for £8,000-worth of shares.

The promoters held their first meeting at Bridgwater on 1 December 1851 and decided to call the company the Somersetshire Central Railway. The Act received Royal Assent on 17 June 1852 and construction started two months later on 16 August. The broad gauge line took advantage of the canal and was built chiefly along, or close to, its bank. Although the land was flat and earthworks caused little difficulty or expense, the contractors were faced with marshy patches where peat bog had been reclaimed from the sea. Layers of bushes, gravel and clay were placed in the holes where the peat had been excavated and on this foundation were placed tree trunks lashed together. Where the bog was particularly soft, floating frames were provided to give a base for the track. Since there were no tunnels, big bridges or earthworks, it proved to be one of the cheapest lines in the kingdom: the total cost, including stations, surveying and Parliamentary expenses, worked out at £6,560 per mile.

The contractors, Messrs Rigby, who had taken a third of the shares, worked quickly, and on 17 August 1854 the completion of the line from Highbridge Wharf to Glastonbury was celebrated, with all the pomp that the Victorians loved on such occasions. About midday, a special train of six coaches carrying railway officials left Highbridge, drawn by B&ER 2–2–2WT No. 33, decorated with flags and flowers. It passed through a triumphal arch of evergreen at Shapwick station, and cannons and bells welcomed it at Glastonbury, reached in about thirty-five minutes. There were flags, banners and a mile-long procession, and a feast was held for over 1,200 people. A thousand workers had tea at Street, and in addition tea and cake were distributed to 1,500 females. The railway opened to the general public on 28 August.

On 3 May 1858 the $1^1/_2$ mile extension from Highbridge to Burnham was opened. Beyond the station a 900 ft long line ran down a pier where vessels could land passengers at any state of the tide, a railway-owned ferry service connecting with Cardiff. The pier line was too steep for locomotive operation and rolling stock was moved up and down by rope and capstan. From 1874 until 1932 the rails on the pier were used by the launching cradle of the lifeboat, brought from its house on a siding.

Highbridge Wharf handled timber from the Baltic ports, rails, coal and so on, while Caerphilly cheese made in Somerset was dispatched to South Wales. S&DR shipping interests ceased in 1934 but until about 1950 the wharf was still used by other vessels.

The Somerset Central Railway built a mixed gauge extension from Glastonbury to the Dorset Central Railway at Bruton, later named Cole, the line being opened on 3 February

1862. When it abolished the broad gauge on 7 August that same year, the two companies united to form the Somerset and Dorset Railway. When the Bath extension was opened in 1874, the Evercreech Junction to Burnham section was reduced to branch status, the Bath to Bournemouth route becoming the main line. The Highbridge branch proved a useful link for many years, until the expansion of road transport after the Second World War made its operation uneconomic. This resulted in the closure of the Highbridge to Burnham section on 29 October 1951, though excursions continued to use the line until 8 September 1962. Evercreech Junction to Bason Bridge closed on 6 March 1966 and Bason Bridge to Highbridge on 3 October 1972, when the dairy milk traffic in bulk tanks ceased.

The S&DJR had its own locomotive and carriage works at Highbridge, which closed in 1930 as an economy measure, throwing 300 men out of work. The works depended entirely on the railway, for no road access was provided. Until 1930, S&DJR locomotives wore their own blue livery, but during that year they were taken into LMS stock and to those uninitiated, it was very surprising to see LMS engines apparently so far from home territory – at Bournemouth for example. Nationalization in 1948 saw another change of livery, but otherwise locomotive types remained as before. Then, in 1958 the Western Region took over the Highbridge line and tested ex-GWR 2251 class 0–6–0s. In 1960 this class started to replace ex-LMS engines that were being scrapped, and the strange coincidence arose of ex-GWR 0–6–0 No. 3218 replacing ex-LMS No. 3218. The 2251 class worked the branch until mid-1963 when passenger trains were in charge of ex-LMS Ivatt Class 2 2–6–2Ts.

A curious accident happened near Ashcott where there were peat workings either side of the track. 19 August 1949 was a foggy morning, and No. 3260 was hauling the 8.00 a.m. mixed train from Glastonbury to Bridgwater when it struck a narrow gauge peat locomotive which had become wedged on a level crossing. No. 3260 was derailed, but the footplatemen jumped clear before the engine and tender fell into the river on the south side of the low embankment. This embankment, being on peat, was insufficiently strong to support the two cranes needed to lift the engine, so it had to be cut up.

Although most railwaymen were honest, there was the odd black sheep. One driver on the branch once stole two ducks from a farm. Their owner, suspecting that an engineman was responsible, reported the matter to the police and two detectives awaited the errant driver at Evercreech Junction. They searched the engine but could find no trace of the missing birds and had to go away empty-handed. And where were the ducks? In their natural element of course – swimming in the tender's water tank!

The public esteem which a railwayman could earn at a country station, is perpetuated in the title of the Peter Mogg Inn at Burtle, the village once served by Edington Junction. The Railway Hotel public house was renamed to commemorate this respected S&DR railwayman whose career started at Edington Junction as porter and continued with thirty years as signalman at the same station. He died in 1963, and was followed in railway service by his son, Maurice, who drove an LMS delivery van at Bath in the thirties. After war service with railway operating companies of the Royal Engineers, Maurice retired at senior inspectorate level from Crewe after forty-five years of service.

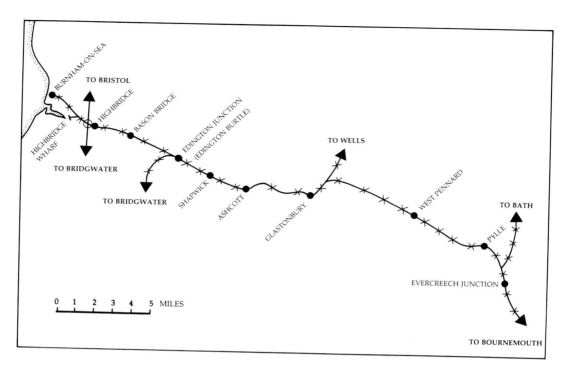

Ex-S&DJR Class 3F 0–6–0 No. 43194 entering Pylle Halt with the 2.20 p.m. Highbridge to Evercreech Junction. The crossing loop was taken out of use on 8 December 1929. Notice the posters on the end wall of the station advertising trips to Burnham-on-Sea, Bournemouth, London, Weston-Super-Mare and Poole. S&DJR village stations on this branch were usually without canopies.

21.8.58 Hugh Ballantyne

The attractive station at West Pennard looking towards Evercreech Junction. Notice the pleasing shrub on the signal box wall, the neat station building and milk churns on both platforms, with three fire buckets hanging on the timber waiting shelter. Beyond is the substantial goods shed. The nearest vehicle is S&DJR Cattle Truck No. 12: like all vehicles of this type, the floor was periodically lime-washed. On the right, notice the neat timber covering above the point rodding.

c. 1905 Author's Collection

Ex-GWR 2201 class 0–6–0 No. 2219 with a train for Evercreech Junction, photographed at West Pennard from the brake van of a passing freight.

28.6.63 Rev. Alan Newman

Flooding of Glastonbury and Street station, looking towards Highbridge. The platform on the right is an island and Wells trains used the right-hand face. Being a principal S&DR station, Glastonbury was supplied with a covered footbridge, whereas at most other branch stations passengers crossed at track level.

1894 Author's Collection

Class 1P 0–4–4T No. 58072 at Glastonbury with an Evercreech Junction to Highbridge train. Built in 1893, she was scrapped in 1956. No. 58072 was fitted with condensing apparatus for working through tunnels in London.

c. 1951 Ian L. Wright

2201 class 0–6–0 No. 2219, of 82G Templecombe shed at Glastonbury, with an Evercreech Junction to Highbridge train. Notice the Morris Commercial Royal Mail van on the platform, with sacks being either loaded on to or taken off the train. The 'T' to the left of the smokebox indicates the termination of a permanent way speed restriction. A row of fire buckets hang on the timber-built signal box.

c. 1958 T.J. Saunders

Ex-S&DJR Class 3F 0–6–0 No. 43216 with the 4 p.m. Highbridge to Evercreech Junction near Glastonbury. The Western Region took over control of the line in 1958 and its influence can be seen in the ex-GWR 'B' set coaches.

1.5.62 David Holmes

The fireman's view from an ex-GWR 2201 class 0–6–0 as it passes the derelict S&DJR's Highbridge Works.

c. 1963 P Strong

The S&DJR Erecting Shop, Highbridge Works.

c. 1900 Author's Collection

The S&DJR Body and Wagon Shop.

c. 1900 Author's Collection

Ex-S&DJR Class 3F 0–6–0 No. 43228 being turned at Highbridge.

22.8.51 Rev. Alan Newman

An ex-GWR 2201 class 0–6–0 and ex-GWR coach stand at Highbridge Platform Three with a train to Evercreech Junction. Five platforms seems an extravagance for a passenger service of only about five trains each way daily. The closed S&DJR works are in the right background.

c. 1963 P. Strong

The two stations at Highbridge: that of the GWR on the main Bristol to Taunton line on the right; the S&DJR station on the left; and the Burnham branch crossing the GWR in the foreground. In the centre is the GWR's Highbridge West signal box.

c. 1920 Author's Collection

The S&DJR terminus at Burnham was of sufficient importance to warrant a train shed; notice its attractive two-coloured valance. The excursion platform, left, did not require any cover as it was normally only used during fine weather. The goods shed, right, has an attractive band of lighter coloured brick. Nine fire buckets hang on the goods shed wall and there are three on the passenger station building.

c. 1910 Author's Collection

Card advertising the Paddle Steamer *Sherbro*, the S&DJR's last steamer on the Burnham to Cardiff crossing.

c. 1887 Author's Collection

Glastonbury to Wells

When the Somerset Central Railway opened between Glastonbury and Highbridge, a new horse omnibus service linked it with Wells, and eventually the line was extended to the city on 3 March 1859. The opening day was declared a general holiday: triumphal arches were erected, houses decorated, evergreens, bunting and flags were in evidence, while the sides of the principal streets were decorated with trees. Among the inscriptions were: 'Success to the Railway,' 'Prosperity to the City of Wells' and 'The Triumph of the Nineteenth Century' – this latter being somewhat of an exaggeration! Two large signs on the Town Hall looked rather curious in juxtaposition: 'The earth is the Lord's and all that therein is' and 'Cheer boys, cheer; there's wealth for honest labour.'

The mayor and council received the directors on the 11.15 a.m. from Highbridge, which was made a special at Glastonbury where the directors boarded for the trip to Wells. There were cheers and, as the train approached the station in Priory Road, a salute from a Russian gun that had been captured in the Crimean War three years before. In the evening fireworks rounded off the day's entertainment.

The village of Coxley submitted two petitions for a station, but the directors turned these down in favour of one at Polsham which was opened two years later.

Although the Somerset Central Railway took over the working of the line from the B&ER on 3 February 1862, the latter still ran a daily passenger train from Bristol to Wells via Highbridge and took 25 per cent of the receipts, the B&ER's Yatton to Wells line not being opened until 1870. This train continued running until October 1868 and was the last broad gauge train to run on the S&DR, the railway having been renamed on 7 August 1862 when the Somerset Central amalgamated with the Dorset Central Railway.

A mile east of Glastonbury, the Wells branch diverged from the main line to Evercreech Junction. Until 2 December 1878 a signal box was situated here, first called Bruton Junction and then Wells Branch Junction. With the closure of the box, an extra track was laid to Glastonbury and what appeared to be an 'Up' and 'Down' line east of Glastonbury, was in reality two single lines.

Approaching Wells, the branch passed the engine shed before reaching the terminal station with its all-over roof, common in Victorian principal stations. The two-road engine shed was pulled down in 1956, having been temporarily closed in April 1935 as the original rails were in very bad condition and needed replacing. The GWR shed at Wells provided temporary hospitality for the engines. A splendid pumping station opened in 1861 and lifted water for locomotive use by means of a water wheel. The S&DR water tank at Wells had a private pipe connection to supply a farm whose water supply was cut off by the diversion of a stream when the branch was built. The crossing keepers at Coxley and Polsham were supplied with water from Wells in 8 gallon cans, trains stopping regularly to drop them off.

Although GWR trains from Yatton to Witham ran through the S&DR station, they did not call until 1 October 1934 and then continued to do so until its closure with the Glastonbury to Wells branch on 29 October 1951. This event was not unexpected as an average of only six passengers used the line daily and the numbers of goods wagons had decreased from eighty to a hundred daily to ten. The engine of the last train was 0–4–4T No. 58086, of a type which had worked over the S&DJR since 1877.

Although trains ceased working from Glastonbury in 1951, Priory Road sidings continued to be used, access being maintained over the former GWR route. They were not taken out of use until 12 October 1964.

Fortunately no serious accident ever occurred on the branch, but about a century ago, when the Wells train had two open wagons loaded with hay unwisely placed between the engine and coaches, a spark from the locomotive set the hay alight just before Polsham. In January 1866 floods at Polsham brought water up to locomotive fireboxes, but did not detain traffic.

In April 1906 the S&DJR hoped to reduce working costs by using a steam railcar, having secured the loan of LSWR No. 1. Despite the presence of an LSWR locomotive inspector to demonstrate firing techniques, steam raising proved a problem. As soon as the fire hole door was opened to feed coal, steam pressure immediately fell; whereas if no coal was fed, likewise pressure dropped. The only solution was to fill the firebox at each station and not fire again until it stopped at the next station. These trials proved that the railcar was unsuited to its duties, and it was returned to the parent company.

In May 1928 four tank engines were equipped for motor train operation. These push-pull trains, usually with a single coach, continued in use until the branch closed.

The largest engine to travel on the Wells branch was the SR 'West Country' class Pacific No. 34092 *City of Wells*, built at Brighton in 1949. It travelled along the branch to its naming ceremony at Wells. This engine is now preserved by the Keighley and Worth Valley Railway.

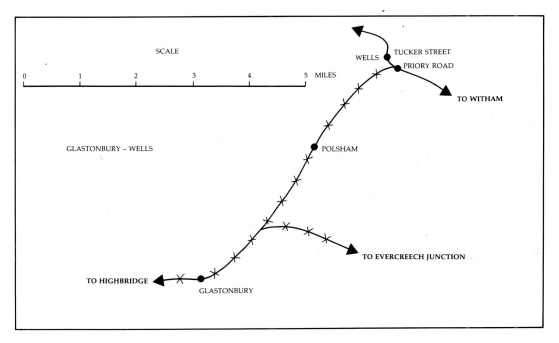

LMS train at Wells: the LMS coach for motor working has 'PL & PH' (pull and push) on its end panel. The engine is in the middle of the train and is hauling a bogie van and four-wheeled van. Wells was of sufficient importance to warrant a train shed. It is of similar design to that at Burnham, but has the luxury of a trough to carry smoke from the interior. Notice the three S&DJR fire buckets, and the gas lamp on a post of old rail.

c. 1935 Lens of Sutton

Motor-fitted Class 1P 0–4–4T No. 58046 at Wells. Built in 1884 she was scrapped in 1951.

10.5.51 Rev. Alan Newman

Motor-fitted Class 1P 0–4–4T No. 1425 at Wells S&DJR shed. When going temporarily to shed the carriage too was taken, to avoid the bother of uncoupling the motor-fitted coach.

c. 1948 Courtesy: Shaw

Standing in front of the S&DJR goods shed at Wells are, left to right, Bill Rawles, fireman; N. Mapstone, porter/guard and Harry Curtis, porter.

c. 1947 Author's Collection

Edington Junction to Bridgwater

When the Somerset Central Railway – later to become one of the partners forming the S&DR – was projected, Bridgwater was put forward as the alternative starting point to Highbridge. The promoters, however, expected to have to tunnel through the Polden Hills and so were deterred on financial grounds. In 1865 the SCR attempted to build a branch line from Shapwick to Bridgwater, but was foiled by the B&ER which promised to lay a third rail from its broad gauge track at Highbridge, through Bridgwater to the LSWR at Yeovil.

The Bridgwater Railway received its Act on 18 August 1882. Nominally independent of the S&DJR, the LSWR agreed to work the line, although to all intents and purposes it was actually worked as part of the S&DJR system of which the LSWR was a partner. The Bridgwater Railway found difficulty in raising capital and this delayed the project, but it eventually became prosperous enough to pay $4^{1}/_{2}$ per cent for many years. Its nominal independence ceased when it was absorbed into the LSWR on 31 December 1922.

The Bridgwater Railway opened on 21 July 1890, a day so wet that a downpour caused the civic reception to be abandoned. As early as 1906 traffic proved light, so LSWR steam railcar No. 1 was tried on this and the Wells branch, but failed to show the expected success. In 1928, as on the Wells branch, motor trains came into operation.

Until the First World War, one or two semi-fast through trains were run between Bridgwater and Templecombe, making London connections there and thus stealing some of the GWR's traffic.

Due to declining traffic, the single coach passenger service was withdrawn on 1 December 1952, and on 1 October 1954 the daily goods from Edington ceased. A connection, however, with Bridgwater North, as the S&DR station had been renamed, was made from the former GWR's docks branch on 27 June 1954, and goods traffic continued to use the station until 7 July 1962.

Closure of the branch created problems for the two women crossing-keepers who always had twenty gallons of water brought by train twice a week to their isolated cottages, and they were forced to make alternative arrangements. Edington station had changed its name to Edington Junction when the Bridgwater Railway opened, and after closure of the branch was altered to Edington Burtle after a hamlet nearer than Edington itself.

Leaving the S&DR at Edington, the single line crossed Chilton Moor and rose at 1 in 72 to a summit at Cossington, followed by a descent at the same gradient to Bawdrip Halt, opened in October 1923. Although 2,185 passengers used it between 7 July and 29 September 1924, it soon suffered from bus competition.

Until its closure in 1942, a line about half a mile in length led from the station past the cement works to a wharf on the River Parrett. Until 1920 a rail-mounted travelling steam crane, built by Thomas Smith of Leeds, was used for lifting at the wharf.

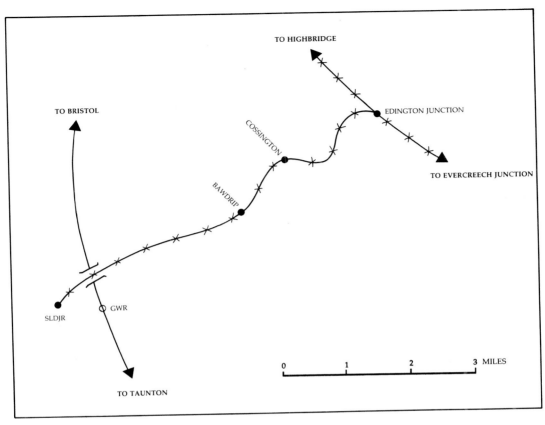

TO HIGHBRIDGE

TO BRISTOL

COSSINGTON

EDINGTON JUNCTION

TO EVERCREECH JUNCTION

BAWDRIP

SLDJR

GWR

TO TAUNTON

0   1   2   3 MILES

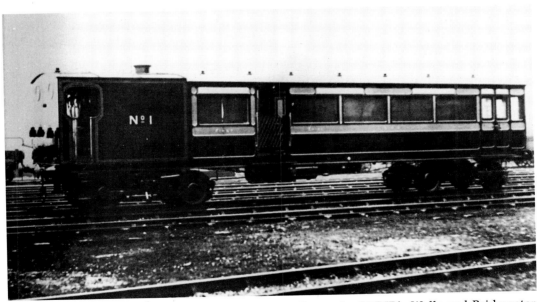

LSWR Railcar No. 1, which was tried experimentally on the S&DJR's Wells and Bridgwater branches.

Author's Collection

Ex-S&DJR Class 3F 0–6–0 No. 43194 standing at Edington Junction bay platform, with a mixed train for Bridgwater. It consisted of a passenger coach and two open wagons, the last carrying a rear lamp on its coupling hook.

c. 1950 M.E.J. Deane

Ex-S&DJR Class 3F 0–6–0 No. 43194 at Cossington with an Edington Junction to Bridgwater train.

c. 1950 M.E.J. Deane

An 0–4–4T approaches Bawdrip Halt with a train from Bridgwater. Shortly after opening in October 1923, a shelter was erected on the platform.

c. 1924 Author's Collection

Ex-S&DJR Class 3F 0–6–0 No. 43194 at Bridgwater. Notice the coal staithes on the left, and the locomotive and turntable pits on the right.

c. 1950 M.E.J. Deane

S&DJR steam crane at Bridgwater Wharf.

c. 1900 Author's Collection

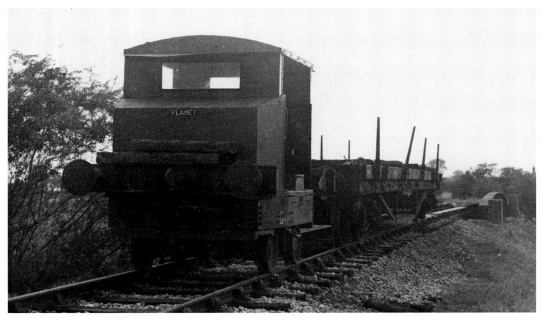

A Planet internal combustion engined locomotive on a demolition train with an ex-GWR bogie bolster for rails. The photograph was taken by the girder bridge just west of Edington Burtle.

29.8.56 Author